Critica[l] ...
the works [of]

MW00416945

Canawlers

"Come 'canawling' with the Fitzgeralds and experience the joys and dangers of life on the C&O Canal. You'll almost hear the horn blowing as they approach another lock."

The Potomac Review

"A powerful, thoughtful and fascinating historical novel, *Canawlers* documents author James Rada, Jr. as a writer of considerable and deftly expressed storytelling talent."

Midwest Book Review

"James Rada, of Cumberland, has written a historical novel for high-schoolers and adults, which relates the adventures, hardships and ultimate tragedy of a family of boaters on the C&O Canal. ... The tale moves quickly and should hold the attention of readers looking for an imaginative adventure set on the canal at a critical time in history."

Along the Towpath

The Rain Man

"*The Rain Man* starts out with a bang and engages the reader with its fast-moving plot."

Beyond 50

"*The Rain Man* is a mystery thriller that races from the first raindrops that began the flooding to its dangerous climax in Wills Creek as it became a raging torrent."

Cumberland Times-News

Between Rail and River

"The book is an enjoyable, clean family read, with characters young and old for a broad-based appeal to both teens and adults. *Between Rail and River* also provides a unique, regional appeal, as it teaches about a particular group of people, ordinary working 'canawlers' in a story that goes beyond the usual coverage of life during the Civil War."

Historical Fiction Review

"*Between Rail and River* arrived yesterday – I finished it today. I couldn't put it down. Great job! ... I enjoyed it thoroughly and I'm looking forward to the next installment."

Gary Petrichick
Author of *Pocket Guide to the Civil War
on the Chesapeake and Ohio Canal*

LOOKING BACK:

True Stories of Mountain Maryland

by
James Rada, Jr.

LEGACY
PUBLISHING

A division of AIM Publishing Group

OTHER BOOKS BY JAMES RADA, JR.

Beast

Between Rail and River

Canawlers

Logan's Fire

My Little Angel

The Rain Man

October Mourning

To Stephanie Long, Jennifer Buchheister and Ray Buchheister, thanks for the help and for the memories.
You all are wonderful.

Portions of this book were previously published in the *Cumberland Times News* and *Allegany Magazine*.

LOOKING BACK: TRUE STORIES OF MOUNTAIN MARYLAND

Published by Legacy Publishing, a division of AIM Publishing Group. Gettysburg, Pennsylvania.
Printed in the United States of America.
First printing: August 2009.

ISBN 978-0-9714599-4-6

Cover design by Stephanie E. J. Long and Jennifer Buchheister

Printed in the United States by Morris Publishing
3212 East Highway 30
Kearney, NE 68847
1-800-650-7888

Library of Congress Control Number: 2009908153

LEGACY
PUBLISHING

315 Oak Lane • Gettysburg, Pennsylvania 17325

Woodie
Sticker

7/28/49

19, 019
air cleaner

Table of Contents

1. City began during a parade 249 years ago 3

2. Russian rrince gave up much to become priest 6

3. The B&O vs. the C&O 10

4. Deaths raise suspicion in community 13

5. The night they drove old Dixie out 16

6. Newspaper editor critical of county official
   killed after scathing article 20

7. Doctor revolt at Western Maryland home, infirmary 27

8. The army invasion of 1894 32

9. Mount Savage's "Merchant King" dies during surgery 38

10. Baltimore to Cumberland, the hard way 41

11. A hidden fortune found in Cumberland home 44

12. Mountain City residents get first look at the big screen 47

13. Halloween a time for revelry 50

14. Police officer mortally wounded in Shantytown 53

15. City was a "Paragon" of the auto industry 59

16. Ridgeley is an example of what a vote means 62

17. Got milk? Get killed 67

18. Queen City leaders brought up on
    bribery charges in scandal of 1914 70

19. Millions "died struggling" with Spanish Flu 73

20. Cumberland's first councilwoman would not serve 79

21. A hand of "Blackjack" 82

22. The Georges Creek mining wars 85

23. How the flood of 1924 all but dried up the C&O Canal ... 90

24. Half-century-old Main Street store destroyed by fire 94

25. The "Babe" comes to Cumberland 97

26. A 10-pound-boy named "Oxygen" 101

27. It wasn't a spaceship that landed at Mexico Farms 104

28. Slot machines have been legal
   in Maryland on two occasions 106

29. All they knew was that it filled their empty bellies 109

30. The French sculptor from Lonaconing 112

31. No overalls in sight: Cumberland
   life surprises city girl from Boston 115

32. Shopping was encouraged because
   shortages lay ahead 119

33. When the World War came to Allegany County 122

34. Family desperately searches for woman's killer 126

35. Trumans draw a crowd in Frostburg during lunch stop .. 132

36. "It's a girl" three times 134

37. Surprise guests 137

38. Crew jumps, B-52 crashes 140

39. After nearly 40 years, Welch
   murder case still unsolved 144

40. Washington a favorite uncle 149

Author's Introduction

Allegany County and Western Maryland have a rich history covering hundreds of years. It's filled with stories of adventurers and Indians, presidents and wars and those ordinary little stories of life past that those of use today have forgotten.

I was lucky enough to begin writing about those stories with my first historical novel, *Canawlers*. While the novel was based on fact, it was a work of fiction. However, my editors at the *Cumberland Times-News* recognized the fact that I had an interest in history and began assigning me stories associated with local history.

Then in 2004, I was offered the chance to begin writing the newspaper's local history column. Needless to say, I jumped at the opportunity. I started browsing through old newspapers looking for stories that caught my attention and a lot of them did.

I start with the newspaper article and from that point, I will research more about the people involved or the situation. If the story is recent enough, I have even been able to interview living participants. The result is another thread in the richly-colored tapestry of this region.

Cumberland Times-News Managing Editor Jan Alderton wrote in his August 1, 2004, newspaper column, "Of the many features we've introduced to Times-News readers in recent years, few have had as much favorable reaction as the Looking Back local history column being written by James Rada.

"The microfilm filed of *Times-News* papers date back to the 1870s and are a goldmine of interesting stories about our past. Some of the stories are ones that present day readers have never heard about. Other stories that Rada is unearthing are about topics that people have talked about for years."

I think part of the success of the column is that I truly enjoy discovering a new story about this area and writing about it. That enthusiasm becomes part of the column and people sense it.

Looking Back: True Stories of Mountain Maryland is a collection of many of the Looking Back columns I have written, but it includes more. This volume includes some of the historical features I wrote for the *Cumberland Times-News* and *Allegany Magazine*. It also includes expanded versions of some of the Looking Back columns.

I hope you enjoy this collection and that you continue to follow my columns and articles in the *Cumberland Times-News* and *Allegany Magazine.*

James Rada, Jr.
June 1, 2009

City began during
a parade 249 years ago

Cumberland was created in the grand spectacle of a parade that happened 249 years ago today.

The *Cumberland Evening Times* reported in 1955, "Two hundred years ago day after tomorrow Cumberland had its first big parade and one that, in all probability, has never been surpassed."

In May 1755, a new fort had recently been completed on the high bluff between the Potomac River and Wills Creek.

It was about 200 yards long and 46 yards wide. Eighteen-foot-long logs that were buried on end 6 feet into the ground and then lashed together made up the walls.

Various armaments, including cannons, were mounted at the top of the walls and slits had been left between some logs in order to fire small arms through the hole at attacking enemies.

This new fort had been built to replace a smaller fort called Mount Pleasant that had been built on the same site in 1754.

Gov. Horatio Sharpe had deemed Mount Pleasant too small for staging an attack on Fort Duquesne in Pennsylvania and had ordered it rebuilt.

Col. James Innes, a South Carolinian, arrived at the fort on Sept. 1, 1754, and took command of a couple of hundred soldiers stationed there. This was a fraction of the army needed to man and defend the larger fort and he and his men waited anxiously for reinforcements.

Gen. Edward Braddock, commander-in-chief of British military forces of North America, was given the job of driving the French from the Ohio Valley.

"On May 10, after an exhausting journey overland, he (Braddock) reached Wills Creek and entered the fort to the booming of cannon,' Gordon Kershaw wrote in *Allegany County: A History.*

Sharpe had given Braddock an elegant chariot to ride in and Braddock rode it much of the way from Winchester. He also rode in it as he entered the fort through the small gates in the north and south walls at the eastern point of the fort.

British Gen. Edward Braddock and his troops, including a young George Washington, arrive at the fort Braddock would name Fort Cumberland on May 10, 1755. Photo courtesy of the Albert and Angela Feldstein Collection.

The soldiers with Braddock were sharply dressed in their scarlet coats and marched in a tight formation. A military band played "The Grenadier March" and other guns were fired in salute at the soldiers marched past the barracks to the parade grounds near the western end of the fort.

Innes greeted Braddock and his staff, among whom was young 23-year-old Virginia colonel named George Washington. Washington had been to the area three times before.

When Braddock was told the new fort had not been named, "One of his first actions upon arrival was to rename the structure for the Duke of Cumberland, soldier-son of George II and Captain General of the British Army," wrote Kershaw.

Fort Cumberland was first written in a letter Braddock wrote to Sharpe on May 22. The fort eventually became the City of Cumberland. With its existence beginning with a parade, it's no wonder that Cumberland residents still enjoy the city's parades.

This article originally appeared in the Cumberland Times-News on May 10, 1004.

Russian prince gave up much to become priest

Demetrius Augustine Gallitzin felt he had already given up so much to become a priest. He'd been a Russian prince living a life of luxury in Europe for most of his life and now he was being asked to go into the wilderness where no one else wanted to go. He was going to Cumberland.

Before he left on his first trip to St. Mary's Church (now St. Patrick's) in 1795, he wrote his mentor Bishop John Carroll, "Your Grace, I am receiving this letter at the moment of my departure for Cumberland. I am very offended that you are insisting on that. I beg you to have a little regard for my feelings. You told me in Baltimore that you would not force me to go to that congregation in the backwoods. Please send your response immediately since I will be returning in 10 days."

From Cumberland to Taneytown was a 175-mile trip in those days before the railroad, the canal or the National Road. The journey had to be made on horseback and Gallitzin left before dawn.

"It took Gallitzin about three days by horse to get to Cumberland each time he visited to bring the sacraments to the people here," said Father Thomas Bevan at St. Patrick's church.

The church where he offered the Mass was a large log cabin on the St. Patrick's property. A plaque marks the site of the original church now. At the time, the church was only four years old. The first Mass had been celebrated there in 1791 by Father Dennis Cahill.

Gallitzin became the second priest to serve at St. Mary's. He would make the three-day journey between Taneytown and Cumberland about once a month. He served St. Mary's from 1795 to 1799.

"By that time, he had so fallen in love with the people in the West that news had come to him of even more people to the northwest of Cumberland who needed the sacraments. Reluctantly, Bishop Carroll told him that he could go," said Bevan.

Gallitzin and a number of Maryland families set off to the north looking for Irish and Germans who were in the Western Pennsylvania wilderness. When he found them, Gallitzin would stay with them for the next 30 years of his life.

"His work flowered, in that even today, that area has one of the highest concentrations of Catholic population in the state of Pennsylvania," said Bevan.

Rev. Demetrius Augustine Gallitzin

Gallitzin's efforts have been so far-reaching that the Diocese of Altoona-Johnstown has recommended to the Pope John Paul II that Gallitzin, "the Apostle of the Alleghenies," be canonized as a saint.

When Gallitzin died on May 6, 1840, he was a poor priest who was beloved by Catholics in Maryland and Pennsylvania. It is a far cry from how he began life as a privileged prince.

7

Gallitzin was born in the Netherlands to a Russian prince and a German countess on December 22, 1770. His godmother was the Empress Catherine the Great of Russia and he was baptized into the Russian Orthodox Church.

In 1787, Gallitzin, influenced by his mother who experienced a resurgence of her Catholic faith, made his first confession and took first communion in the church.

After finishing his education, he was appointed aide-de-camp to the Austrian General von Lillien. There was no opportunity for him to advance in the Austrian army so his parents resolved that he should spend two years traveling through America, the West Indies and other foreign lands. His father knew Benjamin Franklin and John Adams and hoped he would learn from them.

Gallitzin learned from Carroll instead after his arrival in Baltimore on Oct. 28, 1792.

During his travels in America, Gallitzin took the name of Schmet, or Smith, and for many years he was known as Augustine Smith. This allowed him to avoid the inconvenience and expense of traveling as a Russian prince.

During his travels he was impressed by the needs of the church and he resolved to devote his life and fortune to the salvation of souls in America.

"He saw around him many immigrants who wanted to persist in their Catholic faith but were denied in the new world a sufficiency of priests to minister to them. These people had come from a Europe that hated their Catholic faith. They had come to America to be able to practice that faith and here were often denied the consolation of the sacraments for the lack of clergy," said Bevan.

Around that time, there were about 36,000 Catholics in America spread from Canada to Florida and west to the Mississippi River. Carroll was the only bishop in the country and he had only 18 priests to serve his flock.

Gallitzin entered St. Mary's Seminary, which had opened in 1791 in Baltimore, as one of the first students. On March 18, 1795, he was ordained a priest. He was the second ordained priest in America and the first to receive all of the orders from tonsure to priesthood in America.

"Following his ordination to the Catholic priesthood, he was disowned by his family. He lost his title and inheritance. Later in life, Fa-

8

ther Demetrius wrote endless letters to his family in Russia trying to obtain funds to support his missionary activity, all to no avail," said Bevan.

None of this deterred Gallitzin who served with vigor and unselfishness to provide for the spiritual and physical needs of the Catholics in Western Maryland and Pennsylvania.

When Gallitzin died in Loretto, Pa., he was a happy man. Once when his mother had urged him to return to the comforts of Europe, he had written to her, saying, "You can be fully assured that I have no other will in life, and wish to have no other, than that of fulfilling God's will. You can be further assured that I find no lasting joy outside of the activities of my calling."

This article originally appeared in the Cumberland Times-News on August 23, 2004.

The B&O vs. the C&O

It was a race from the very beginning. The winner would survive and loser would perish.

On July 4, 1828, President John Quincy Adams broke ground for the Chesapeake and Ohio Canal near Great Falls, Md. On the same day, Charles Carroll, the last living signer of the Declaration of Independence broke ground for Baltimore and Ohio Railroad, in Baltimore just 40 miles away.

Their destination?

Cumberland, and then as both the business names suggest, Ohio and beyond.

The first clash between the two occurred in the courts when the B&O claimed a right of way through Point of Rocks, an area of Maryland between the mountains and the Potomac River that had room for the canal or the railroad, but not both. The C&O owned the right of way through its charter, but the railroad had gathered up permission from the landowners to build.

"It [the railroad] had aggressively gathered land waivers in the narrowed valley where it knew very well that usurpation would provoke a head-on collision with the canal company. Its grab did indeed precipitate showdown time, and the canal and railroad fought it out in the courts for four years," Elizabeth Kytle wrote in *Home on the Canal*.

Though the C&O won that case, the delay nearly bankrupted the company. The B&O continued to fight through the courts with injunctions and high demands for rights of way.

On site, both the railroad and canal companies fought for workers, seeking to lure them away from each other.

The B&O won the race to Cumberland, arriving eight years before the canal opened, giving the railroad a significant advantage in establishing itself.

The companies then began to fight for freight. At one point, the B&O raised its rates to haul flour and encouraged the C&O to do so as well. When the canal company did, the railroad reduced its rates to even lower than they had been originally. Within a few months, the B&O had virtually put the C&O out of the flour-hauling business.

Tension between the two companies showed itself in day-to-day operations as well. At the points along the routes where the canal and the railroad run side by side, engineers were known to blow their whistles to spook the mules on the towpath and cause problems for the canallers.

At the places where the canal and railroad ran side by side, railroaders liked to blow their whistles to spook the canal mules. Courtesy of the National Park Service.

The C&O Canal was in a constant struggle for its existence and never fulfilled its ultimate goal of connecting to the Ohio River. However, the B&O Railroad did see success and continued to expand, including buying a stake in the canal.

When the flood of 1889 washed out the canal and put it in receivership, the B&O Railroad took over its rival and began to run it. While the railroad would have like to just shut down the canal operation, it couldn't. Though the canal itself was a financial burden on the railroad, the B&O Railroad could use the canal rights of way to block other railroads from coming into the area. The courts had ordered that the railroad needed to operate the canal profitably or lose its charter. If that happened, other railroads could have gotten a foothold in Western Maryland.

George Hooper Wolfe, wrote in *I Drove Mules on the C&O Canal*, "The railroad saw in this an opportunity to relieve itself of the expense of further operation. Enough repairs were made to assert that the Canal was a going concern, with enough revenues from the Georgetown factories and dams along the river to pay the expenses of a minimum operating staff; and it was also maintained that the Canal could be placed in operation quickly if business warranted. The court went along with this fiction, and the B&O retained the property, but without having any further expenses for its maintenance."

And so the B&O continued to operate the canal until the flood of 1924 put the canal out of business permanently. The B&O sold its rights to the canal to the federal government in August 1938 for $2 million.

Otho Swain was born on the canal in 1901 and worked on it during its final years. He said in a 1976 interview, "The canal finally closed down in 1924. There was flood damage then, but the railroad—it was the railroad that really killed the canal."

This article originally appeared in the Cumberland Times-News on June 30, 2008.

Deaths raise suspicion in community

Even as Mrs. Samuel Engle brought a new life into the world, her own death had been sealed by the woman who was supposed to care for her.

The year was 1851 and Engle had gone into labor in her home near Grantsville. Her personal nurse, Nancy Hufferd, assisted her through the birth. Nancy and Mrs. Engle were alone in the bedroom as the expectant mother thrashed and sweated on the bed with each contraction.

Nancy walked to the wash basin and poured water into a cup that sat next to the basin. Then she added something extra to the cup of water. That extra was arsenic. She soaked a towel in the water and wrung it out. She carried it back to the woman on the bed and wiped the sweat from her face.

"It won't be long now, Mrs. Engle," Nancy said. "Here drink some water. It will help you."

Mrs. Engle obeyed and Nancy smiled.

The baby was eventually born, but Mrs. Engle never recovered from the effects of childbirth. Sam Engle wondered why his wife wasn't getting better. The delivery had gone smoothly and was not unusual in any way, Nancy assured him.

Barely a week after the birth of the baby, Mrs. Engle died.

"Suspicions at once arose in and out of the Engle mansion that there had been foul play," wrote the *Cumberland Evening Times* in a 1907 article about the case.

Among the believers that Mrs. Engle was a victim of foul play was her physician, J.H. Patterson. He performed an autopsy on her body but could find no evidence of any poison.

"She was buried in due time, but the belief and excitement spread over the whole neighborhood, which led to the disinterment of the woman, and a second post-mortem examination was made by Drs. Patterson, Hermann and J.J. Bruce, who had just commenced the practice," wrote the *Cumberland Evening Times*.

The stomach was sent to Professor Atkin in Baltimore for examination. In the meantime, Nancy was arrested and placed in the Allegany County Jail in September. In October, she was indicted in Allegany County Circuit Court since Grantsville was still part of Allegany County at that time.

The trial began in November before Judge Wiesel. State's Attorney James Schley and Frank Thomas prosecuted the case. T.I. McKaig and George Pearre defended Nancy.

During the trial, 23 witnesses were called, including five doctors. The state's evidence was called circumstantial. It rested on the fact that Nancy had purchased a lot of arsenic from a store in Grantsville with the remark that she wanted to make a salve for her sore leg. Prosecutors pointed out that she never had a sore leg.

On the other side of the table, the poison could not be found, and Professor Atkin testified that he had found no arsenic in Engle's stomach.

"Who can say the verdict would have been the same if the remaining poison had been produced at the trial? She was acquitted according to the rules of law; but there was hardly one in the whole neighborhood believed her to be innocent," wrote the *Cumberland Evening Times*.

The arsenic Nancy purchased eventually was found hidden in a bureau in the Engle house after the trial had ended.

This spurred people to look more into why Nancy had been widowed three times. Two of her four husbands died under mysterious circumstances.

Her first husband was John Yeast, a strong, healthy man who died "unexpectedly, if not mysteriously" in 1834, according to the *Cumberland Evening Times*. There were suspicions at the time that the death wasn't from natural causes, but it wasn't followed up on.

John Layman was Nancy's second husband. He was a respectable and prominent citizen in the community and died from cancer in 1845.

Philip Hufferd of Somerset County was husband No. 3, but he died suddenly after eating a pumpkin pie not too long before Mrs. Engle died. Again, the husband's death caused suspicion but no one took action.

Her fourth husband was Holmes Wiley, but Hufferd died before she could be widowed again.

The *Cumberland Evening Times* noted that Nancy never had a child and "She is remembered by only a few and cared for by none, it may be said."

This article appeared in the Cumberland Times-News on May 24, 2004.

The night they drove old Dixie out

During the Civil War, towns changed hands depending on which army was nearest. Romney went back and forth between Union and Confederate control more times than you can count on your fingers and toes. Boonsboro didn't even wait for a demand to surrender. It flew the flag of whatever army was nearest.

But Cumberland always flew the Stars and Stripes throughout the entire 1,500-odd days (depending on when you consider the beginning and end of the war) of the Civil War.

Except for one day.

On June 16, 1863, the Union Army in Cumberland totally pulled out of the city to concentrate their forces at New Creek, which is now known as Keyser. The Union forces were gathering to oppose General Robert E. Lee's Army, which was expected to push into Maryland.

While Gen. Lee did cross into Maryland, the crossing was made at Williamsport as the Confederates marched in their way to Gettysburg.

When the Union Army left Cumberland, the Baltimore and Ohio Railroad took all of its rolling stock and light machinery and sent it north.

With no military defense, the city residents were hysterical, expecting the Confederate Army to march on them at any time.

"On the 16th, it was reported that the enemy was rapidly approaching the city in force, whereupon a number of citizens retired with considerable precipitancy in the direction of Pennsylvania, and merchants began to cast about for means whereby they might save their goods from confiscation by unexpected visitors. The next morning strangers were seen out on Williams Road," James Thomas and Thomas Williams wrote in the *History of Allegany County*.

Night fell and Cumberland remained untaken.

The next morning strangers and artillery pieces were seen on Williams Road outside of town. Two cavalrymen who had escaped from the destruction of Maj. General Robert Milroy's command at Winchester a few days earlier approached the strangers and were fired upon by two cannon. The cavalrymen quickly retreated.

Frightened citizens took refuge and merchants closed up their stores. Other groups of citizens gathered in the street to see what would happen.

Shortly thereafter, two Confederates entered town and walked down Baltimore Street under the white flag of truce. Acting Mayor Valentine A. Buckey and a group of citizens met them under a flag of truce.

The Confederate soldiers handed Buckey a note addressed to the military commander of Cumberland from Colonel George W. Imboden of the 18th Virginia Cavalry. The letter read: "You are surrounded by a superior force, and as an act of humanity, I demand the surrender of the city. The bearer, Captain R.B. Muses, is authorized to negotiate as to terms of surrender."

Buckey wrote out his reply and gave it to Muses. His letter to Imboden read: "Sir: Your note addressed to officer commanding at this point has just been handed to me, and as there is no force here to resist you, and no officer in command, I, as Mayor, for the time being, do as far as I can, surrender the city as demanded, upon the following terms, viz: That private persons and property, and the property of the State of Maryland, be respected."

Imboden's written reply was: "Sir: I will receive a surrender of the City of Cumberland, and will respect all private property except such property as the Quartermaster may desire for the Confederate States. No public property except of the State of Maryland will be respected."

About 350 of Imboden's Cavalry took possession of Cumberland. Their first priority was to secure fresh horses. The soldiers and convinced the merchants to open their stores.

"The Confederates then purchased pretty freely such articles as hats, boots, shoes, clothing, etc., paying for the same in Confederate money, a species of currency which had then rather limited value,"

Union Brig. Gen. Benjamin Kelley's men captured some of the Confederate forces of Col. George Imboden that took over Cumberland for a day. Courtesy of Wikimedia Commons.

wrote Thomas and Williams.

While the soldiers respected most property, they did tear down the telegraph lines and remove train track.

The *Valley News Echo* reported, "The conduct of the Confederates throughout was gentlemanly. They were well-clothed, armed and mounted, and exhibited in no respect evidence of starvation or raggedness."

The Confederates knew a large Union force was in New Creek so they remained in Cumberland for only three hours, leaving by 10:30 a.m.

When they left the city, a few residents who were sympathetic to the Southern cause also went with them. Among these young men were Thomas Black, Lewis Rice and James Thomas, according to Harold Scott in *The Civil War Era in Cumberland, Maryland.*

Brig. General Benjamin Kelly and his staff had passed through Cumberland shortly before the Confederate forces had arriving. When the train they were on reached a torn up area of track and couldn't continue, the train headed back to Cumberland to switch the train onto an alternate route. Kelly's forces arrived back shortly after the Confederates had left. In fact, Kelly's soldiers captured a few of Imboden's men who had remained behind with friends in Cumberland.

The Union Army also found that the B&O Railroad and the Chesapeake and Ohio Canal had been damaged. It took more than a month to restore the telegraph communications because the damage Imboden's men had done.

"*The Richmond Enquirer* told of 'millions of dollars worth of damage done at Cumberland; and Baltimore and Pittsburgh papers dolefully announced a great disaster in Cumberland," wrote David Dean in *Allegany County-A History.*

The only casualty of the capture of Cumberland was Griffin Twigg, a farmer who lived near Murley's Branch.

"The particulars are not known, but the old man was killed; not, however, until he had killed two of the enemy and wounded another," William Lowdermilk wrote in *History of Cumberland.*

The graveyard where the Confederate soldiers are supposedly buried was located by the Genealogical Society in the 1980's near the Meadow Wood Sportsman Club.

This article originally appeared in Allegany Magazine in March 2007.

Newspaper editor critical of county official killed after scathing article

Lloyd Clary of Frostburg was the managing editor of the *Cumberland Daily Times*. He, along with John Broydrick, also owned the newspaper, which was a merging of the *Mountain City Times* and the *Cumberland Times and Civilian*.

On October 27, 1873, Clary wrote an article critical of how the long-time Clerk of the Circuit Court of Allegany County Horace Resley paid jurors.

"The talesmen from Lonaconing were paid $8.50 each; those from Frostburg $4.00 (the Clerk taking the trouble to tell them in Court to go down to the office and get their certificates), while those from Mount Savage and the country districts were allowed to go without being paid at all, and without receiving any intimation from anybody that anything was due them," Clary wrote in the *Cumberland Daily Times*. In addition, Resley was overpaying those jurors he did pay more than they were due.

Further, Clary intimated there was more wrongdoing, perhaps even shady dealings, by writing, "In the case of Lonaconing the money was handed over to Mr. Patrick Mullen, an earnest satellite of the present incumbents, for distribution all of which gives rise to considerable comment."

While it's not known how Horace Resley reacted to the article, his eldest son, John, took it as an attack on his family's honor.

Around 2 p.m. on Oct. 27, an angry John Resley headed for the offices of the *Cumberland Daily Times*. He found Broydrick at the corner of Baltimore and George Streets in front of King's Shoe Store.

"Did you write that article about my father in this morning's paper?" Resley asked.

"No," Broydrick replied.

Resley raised his arm as if he was going to strike Broydrick.

"I don't want any trouble with you," Broydrick said quickly. "I'm no politician."

"I'll make a politician out of you and Clary, too."

Then Resley headed down Baltimore Street to the newspaper office. He found Daniel Bradley, a collector for the newspaper, at the office and asked him if Clary was in. Bradley said he was and Resley headed up the stairs to where Clary's office was located on the second floor.

Resley was in Bradley's sight the entire time, but he was unable to see or hear Clary when the editor met Resley near the top of the stairs.

"I looked after him," Bradley told a jury later. "Just as he reached the top, he put his hand behind him and pulled a revolver and said, 'You son of a—, did you write the article about my father?' Then he fired the two shots, turned about and came down stairs, holding the revolver in his hand."

Both shots struck Clary. One shot hit him in the ribs and was not fatal. However, the other shot went in the left side of Clary's throat, passing through his windpipe and severing his carotid artery as it passed out the side his neck.

Bradley ran up the stairs and found Clary lying on the floor bleeding. Doctors Orr and Dougherty were brought in to try and help him. They stabilized Clary and had him taken on a stretcher to City Hospital.

Before removing him from the newspaper office, Clary made a dying statement to Justice of the Peace J.M. Beall that would be admitted as evidence in Resley's trial. Clary told Beall pretty much the same thing that Bradley would later testify. However, he added that once he had been shot the first time, he told Resley, "Give me a chance." Clary said Resley said, "You damned, son of a bitch, I'll kill you." and then fired the second shot.

Clary's family in Frostburg was notified and they made the half hour trip to Cumberland to be with Clary. A local priest gave Clary the rights of baptism before he died at 8:45 p.m.

Clary was buried two days later, but the story was far from over.

A view of Baltimore Street around the time the editor of the Cumberland Daily Times was killed in the newspaper office in 1873. Courtesy of the National Archives.

Pen kills what the sword couldn't

They say, "The pen is mightier than the sword" and for Lloyd Clary that certainly proved true. The young newspaper editor of the *Cumberland Daily Times* had survived the bullets and swords of the Civil War only to be felled because of something he wrote on October 27, 1873.

"Never in our experience have we been called upon to publish the details of an occurrence more truly painful and shocking than that of the killing of Lloyd Lowndes Clary, the brave editor of the Cumberland Daily Times by John H. Resley..." the *Hagerstown Mail* reported after the murder.

It was in the offices of the newspaper on Oct. 27, that John Resley shot Clary twice, once in the neck and once in the body. The neck shot would kill Clary later that evening.

Though Resley left the scene of his crime, he did not flee. He walked across Baltimore Street and stood on the opposite side looking at the newspaper office. "A considerable crowd gathered around Mr. Resley while be stood on the street. He was very pale and much excited, and moved about nervously. He did not seem inclined to converse, and several times rebuffed persons who spoke to him," reported the Hagerstown Mail.

Eventually Cumberland Police Officer Magruder saw Resley and approached him.

"Am I wanted?" Resley asked.

"Yes you are," Magruder told him and arrested him.

Resley was later indicted for Clary's murder.

While the newspapers detested Resley's actions, they seemed to understand the reasons behind it. The *Hagerstown Herald and Torch* noted that, "It is a fact that the editor referred to wielded a caustic pen, and his paper, as long as we received and read it, contained some terribly severe articles against political opponents."

As with many men of his time, Clary had not been afraid of a fight. He was a Confederate veteran of the Civil War. "Mr. Clary was intensely Southern in his feelings, every pulsation of his young heart beating in unison with the late struggle of the seceding States for their guaranteed and Constitutional rights," one obituary noted.

He had joined McNeill's Rangers in 1862. The *Hagerstown Mail* credits Clary for planning and executing the kidnapping of Union Generals George Crook and Benjamin Kelley from a hotel on Baltimore Street in February 1865.

"Young Clary in company with four others, captured the Federal pickets, dashed into Cumberland and at three o'clock in the morning surprised Generals Crook and Kelley, and brought them safely out," the newspaper reported.

Both generals were taken to Richmond where they were paroled and exchanged for Confederate Brigadier General Isaac Trimble.

Crook would later say, "Gentlemen, this is the most brilliant exploit of the war!"

After the war, Clary was a reporter and then editor of the *Mountain City Times*, which merged with the *Cumberland Times and Civilian* to become the *Cumberland Daily Times* in May 1872.

"From its first note to its last the Times has not uttered one uncertain sound. It had but one voice—that of condemnation and exclusion from office of the men whom it had convinced of betrayal of their trusts. Thus fighting he fell with his harness on, a martyr to the cause of honesty, truth and Justice," the *Cumberland Daily Times* noted in its obituary of Clary.

Though there was no question in anyone's mind that Resley had killed Clary, there were still unanswered questions that would come to light during the trial that changed how everyone looked at the murder.

The villain becomes the hero after day in court

On October 27, 1874, John Resley, son of the clerk of the circuit court of Allegany County, shot and killed Lloyd Clary, the editor of the *Cumberland Daily Times* and a Confederate Civil War hero. It appeared to be an open-and-shut case. After all, Resley had confessed to the shooting.

However, just as a battle plan becomes obsolete as soon as the enemy is engaged, so too, go jury trials once the court is called to order.

Resley's murder trial began on January 29, 1874, barely three months after the murder.

The importance of the case was evident in the fact that Maryland Governor William Pinkney Whyte sent the state's attorney general Andrew Syester to assist Allegany County State's Attorney William Reed with the prosecution.

The defense had four attorneys. Col. Charles Marshall of Baltimore was the lead attorney and James M. Schley, J. J. McHenry and William Price, all of the Cumberland bar were assisting.

Chief Justice Alvey, Associate Justice Motter and Associate Justice Pearre presided over the trial.

Reed gave the opening statement for the prosecution at the trial saying "they would prove, he thought, that Resley had not read the article when he committed the act," according to the Hagerstown Mail.

However, the most damning piece of evidence Reed said would be that Resley had confessed in front of witnesses. While standing on Baltimore Street, Resley said, "Nobody else would do it and I did it."

What Reed was starting to do was lay out a case of premeditated murder based not on a newspaper article, but on Resley's hatred for Clary.

Schley deferred giving an opening statement to the jury until the state had made its case.

Among the witnesses called was another *Cumberland Daily Times* editor named Thomas McCardle. On hearing shots fired, McCardle has rushed down from the pressroom and seen Clary holding his throat. "He leaned against the wall as if completely exhausted, his body trembling as if from the effort to keep his feet, holding his throat by one hand, and with the other arm hanging down, holding a pistol in that hand," the newspaper reported.

McCardle testified that he had never seen Resley with a pistol before then. The defense went further to suggest that Clary could have seen Resley coming from a window and gone to get the pistol.

Clary had said in his statement he had been shot without being given a chance and he said as much to Resley just before the man shot him the second time. Clary said he hadn't been able to get his pistol out to return fire.

Schley presented conflicting testimony that Clary had drawn his pistol and furthermore medical evidence showed that Clary wouldn't have been able to say anything immediately after being shot in the throat as Clary said in his own statement.

A later witness would testify that Clary had hurried him out of his office just before rushing out to meet Resley on the stairs. This same witness had heard Clary and Resley argue, Clary's pistol misfire and then two shots from Resley. Resley hadn't gone to the office seeking to kill Clary. Resley had shot him in self defense.

Other witnesses testified that Clary had hated Resley and said, "if ever he crossed his path again he would fill him as full of holes as a net," the newspaper summarized Clary saying about Resley at one time.

After two days of testimony, the jury retired for six hours before returning a verdict of not guilty.

"Resley was then escorted home by the crowd, cheering all the way," the New York Times reported.

Resley would live to be 73 years old and die from a stroke in January 1916.

These articles appeared in the Cumberland Times-News on January 26, 2009; February 2, 2009 and February 9, 2009.

Doctor revolt at Western Maryland Home, Infirmary

In 1893, Dr. G. L. Carder, surgeon-in-chief, for the Western Maryland Hospital needed to operate on a patient, but he couldn't find a doctor in town who would administer the chloroform to the patient. On another case of Carder's, when a woman died after a particularly difficult surgery, other doctors started rumors that Carder had been guilty of malpractice. So prevalent were the rumors that the body had to be exhumed to clear Carder's name.

It wasn't that Carder was a bad surgeon. Far from it. He had graduated from Baltimore Medical College in 1892 at the top of his class. He had come to the forerunner of the Western Maryland Health System with glowing recommendations.

"He was a young man on the threshold of life, who had the highest recommendations, and the board would not be justified in taking him by the neck and heels and throwing him out in the street without good grounds," said George Pearre, hospital superintendent, in the *Cumberland Evening Times*.

The problem was Carder had come here. He wasn't from Cumberland and he didn't live in Cumberland or Allegany County once he did come here.

And for that sin of birth, the doctors in town had banded together to force Carder out of the top medical slot of the hospital.

The Western Maryland Hospital had been around since 1888 when the Maryland legislature passed an act that established the Western Maryland Home and Infirmary for the Aged.

"The facilities were initially located in private homes. The need was realized for a larger facility that would provide hospital care for the large number of railroad accident victims," wrote Al Feldstein in *Postcard Views of Allegany County, Maryland*

A new building on Baltimore Avenue was opened in 1892 and the name eventually became Western Maryland Hospital. It would become Memorial Hospital in 1929 and the Western Maryland Health System in 1996.

In January 1894, a group of doctors traveled to Annapolis to meet with the Governor Frank Brown and members of the legislature.

According to a report in the *Cumberland Evening Times*, Dr. M. A. F. Carr told the governor, "Send a joint committee to Cumberland and investigate the institution. Then we will convince you that the men and women who control its management should be turned out of office. We will show you things that you little dream of!"

The other doctors in the group were G. H. Carpenter, Spear, Porter, Hodgson, Craigen, Doemer, Dukes, Wiley, Greenweil and Fogtmann and they were all dissatisfied with the management of the hospital, in particular, with Carder. However, the governor had the power to appoint the majority of the board of directors to the hospital and the legislature had the ability to cut off the primary source of hospital funding. The Western Maryland Home and Infirmary had received two payments from the state – $5000 in 1890 and $10000 in 1894. For change to happen, the Governor Brown and legislature would have to be convinced.

"I wouldn't send a patient of mine there to be at the mercy of an inexperienced surgeon, and then not be allowed to enter the institution myself," Carr reportedly told the governor in the *Cumberland Evening Times* article.

"Would you be refused admission?" the governor asked.

"They have said that once a patient enters there he is beyond outside control."

"Has any doctor ever applied for admission?"

The newspaper reported that Carr admitted "that no such application had been made, and no self-respecting physician could afford to make it under the circumstances."

This left Governor Brown with a choice to make: Should he reorganize the Western Maryland Home and Infirmary Board of Directors in order to have one physician dismissed or should he allow the directors to make the decision they were appointed by him to make?

The Western Maryland Hospital, located on Baltimore Avenue, circa 1909, is shown in this postcard image. Courtesy of the Albert and Angela Feldstein Collection.

Charity was lacking at WM Home and Hospital

Thought the Western Maryland Home and Hospital in Cumberland was by and large a charity hospital, charity was lacking there in 1894 for at least one doctor, G. L. Carder.

A group of doctors had petitioned Governor Frank Brown to remove Carder as surgeon-in-chief at the hospital in January.

Three weeks later, following the publication of the meeting, a group of businessmen from Cumberland traveled to Annapolis to have their own meeting with the governor and legislature. This group included: George Pearre, an ex-state senator and manager of the hospital; B. S. Randolph, superintendent of the Consolidated Coal Company, C. J. Orrick, wholesale grocer; J. N. M. Brandler, orphans court judge; P. H. Daughtrey, wholesale grocer; David Sloan, Lonaconing Savings Bank;

Henry Rehs, magistrate; Merwin McKaig, president of McKaig Shafting Works; John Avirett, *Cumberland Evening Times* editor; E. J. Cooney, merchant; Willie Cooney, son of E. J. Cooney; T. S. Kean, tax collector and William Shepherd, president of the Third National Bank of Cumberland.

Pearre told the governor that the doctors who had come to Annapolis in January wouldn't tell Pearre what sorts of charges they had leveled against the management. However the doctors did claim they had been misrepresented in the newspaper.

"But, knowing that reporters, while they may not get all that is said, generally are accurate in what they do get, and, further, that the various newspapers agreed as to what took place, I had faith in the published reports," Pearre told the governor as reported in the *Cumberland Evening Times*.

The group's request of the governor was that the current management of the hospital be maintained, the hospital get its normal governmental appropriation and grant a special appropriation to pay off the hospital's debt.

Brown told the group what the doctors had charged against the hospital. He then said he wouldn't make a decision either way until he visited the hospital in April.

"The charges made while without the slightest foundation in fact, might do some harm if we did not refute them before our request for continuance of our appropriation comes before the Legislature. After this vicious act on the part of the physicians, it appeared that all had been postponed until April but we want to contradict the charges before they go any further," Pearre was reported to have said.

He further went on to tell the governor that none of the local doctors had been appointed surgeon-in-chief because none of them had applied for the position. So the board of directors had sought a doctor outside of the area and Carder had come highly qualified. Even then, Pearre said that the hospital still wanted local input.

"We wanted the Cumberland doctors to form a consulting staff to aid Carder, but, instead, they formed, as one of my colleagues wittily said, an 'insulting staff.' Since then the work of the Institution has been misrepresented," Pearre said.

The doctors formed an association opposed to the hospital management and demanding changes that the board thought was a usurpation of the hospital authority, such as control of the nurses at the hospital.

Apparently, someone had a change of heart about Carder between February and April. On April 18, the *Cumberland Evening Times* reported that the board of directors of the Western Maryland Home and Infirmary asked for Carder's resignation.

"At the investigation it was found that Dr. Carder bad failed to be present at an operation, which was to have taken place at the 'Home.' Dr. Carder will tender his resignation within the next sixty days, the time granted him according to his contract with the institution," reported the *Cumberland Evening Times*.

Even on his way out, Carder still proved he was a more-than-capable surgeon. In May, the *Cumberland Evening Times* reported the story of Lewis Davis of Barton. The young boy took ill and began losing weight. At Easter, he weighed only 18 pounds and couldn't speak. Area doctors "pronounced the case of the little fellow hopeless." Lewis was admitted to the Western Maryland Home and Hospital as a last-ditch effort. On May 19, the newspaper reported that Lewis was as "agile as a kitten" and his weight was up to 25 pounds. The reason for his recovery was that Carder had diagnosed the boy's illness and removed a rib from him, which was apparently the source of the problem.

This article appeared in the Cumberland Times-News on August 4, 2008 and August 5, 2008.

The army invasion of 1894

On April 14, 1894, the invasion the residents of Frostburg had been expecting for weeks happened. Coxey's Army appeared at the crest of Federal Hill and marched into town right down Main Street.

"At 4:15 p.m., the marshal of the marching group, a four piece band, flags and banners, and some wagons, followed by a group of 245 tired and bedraggled mortals, crossed Federal Hill and marched in a more or less soldierly fashion down Main Street into Frostburg," Harold Scott wrote in his book *Incredible, Strange, Unusual...*

Coxey's Army was a group of unemployed workers that had formed in Massillon, Ohio, under the direction of Jacob Coxey. The official name of the group was the Commonweal of Christ, but most people referred to it as Coxey's Army. The group planned to march to Washington D.C. where Coxey would present his petition to Congress of his ideas for a national program of building and repairing roads that would also solve the national unemployment problem. The group has started its march with much fanfare, leaving Massillon on Easter Sunday, March 25, and had since then made their way slowly eastward.

"Stories of pillaging, disorderly conduct, and even assaults by the band of men all served to alarm the local residents and spread fear and apprehension as to what the impending invasion would bring. Some news accounts were reporting that the army was infested with drunks, crooks, and toughs," Scott wrote.

While the actual situation was not that bad, the army did face deprivation and slow passage on the very roads they hoped to repair. Infighting over leadership of the group had led to factions forming within it and even a mutiny as the two leaders vied for control of the army.

Carl Browne, who had been appointed by Coxey to lead the group, was ousted from leadership and a group led by Unknown Smith took control. No one knew the man's name and he refused to give it to reporters so they called him "Unknown Smith."

As Coxey's Army marched toward Washington in 1894, they passed through Garrett and Allegany Counties. Courtesy of the Library of Congress.

Dismissed from the group, Browne reached Frostburg first. Though the group was named after Coxey, he rarely traveled with it. Instead he traveled ahead and slept in rooms while the men who followed him were generally forced to sleep outside. Browne's first move on reaching Frostburg was to telegraph Coxey about the incident. Reporters waiting for the army to arrive learned of what had happened and word spread of the mutiny.

So it was when the army marched through town, the city officials were expecting trouble, according to John Grant in his monograph, *Coxey's 38-Day March Through the Alleghenies in Search of Econom-*

ic Justice.

A week before the army's arrival, the Frostburg City Council voted to spend $100 to help accommodate the group. On the day of the army's arrival, citizens took up a collection to feed them and arrangements were made to allow them to sleep in Ravenscroft's Opera House. The city also hired special police officers to help maintain order should the rumors of rowdiness prove to be true.

The expected violence didn't happen when the army arrived. The marchers were tired and hungry. Some suffered from exposure.

The group dubbed the Frostburg stop as Camp Robert E. Lee and started campfires in a vacant lot near the opera house and cooked their evening meals. When the evening shows were over in the opera house, the men went to their accommodations on the third floor.

The following day Coxey arrived from Cumberland to settle the authority dispute between Browne and Smith.

He first praised the group for their efforts to date and added, "The eyes of sixty-five million people are fixed on this noble and patriotic band, and on the success of our movement depends the future happiness of a great people," according to the *Cumberland Evening Times.*

He then called for got a vote to expel from Smith from the group. Browne was restored and the march was ready to continue. Despite their troubles and trials on the march, most of the men still shared Coxey's vision to change government policy.

Coxey's Army left Frostburg at 9 a.m. and headed for Cumberland.

The visit of Coxey's Army

Coxey's Army fought in no war. The men wore no uniforms nor called themselves soldiers. They were unemployed workers named after their leader Jacob Coxey. They marched on Washington in 1894 looking to change national policy. In that single battle, which they sought, they lost, but in the long run, they won the war.

The route of that march on Washington brought the army through Allegany County and Cumberland where the army became a navy.

Coxey's Army left Frostburg at 9 a.m. on April 15 and arrived at Camp Victory around noon. Camp Victory was a Narrows Park baseball field just outside of the city. According to *The Cumberland Evening Times,* the day's weather was beautiful and brought out hundreds

Jacob Coxey later in life. Courtesy of the Library of Congress.

of spectators to watch the army arrive.

"The ball field had a fence around it, which created a chance to collect an admission fee to see the army in camp. This had been done successfully at the Exposition Park near Pittsburgh. On Sunday, April 15, 1500 citizens of Cumberland paid 10 cents to see the army prepare its camp in the ball park," John Grant wrote in his monograph, *Coxey's 38-day March Through the Alleghenies in Search of Economic Justice.*

Cumberland residents contributed food to the army that included six barrels of corn, 10 bales of hay, three quarters of beef, 600 loaves of bread, 140 pounds of bologna, 75 pounds of cheese and 60 pounds of coffee.

Harold Scott wrote in his book *Incredible, Strange, Unusual...*, "...some of the news accounts from Cumberland, noted that although there were some earnest, good men within the army who were out of work and seeking some intervention or program by the Federal Government that would insure jobs in the future, if those spectators who visited the park in the Narrows in Cumberland expected to find a large body of men, with a glorious mission, men determined to stand by their principals at all cost, they no doubt were disappointed. For the most part all they found was a sorry looking bunch of weary, footsore humans, who had very little idea of what their glorious mission and objectives were in marching."

The men rested for the rest of the day at the camp and all through the next day. The time was used to repair equipment, mend clothing, and get haircuts. Scott wrote that during a morning baseball game, "The Working Men" defeated "The Hobos."

Behind this much-needed rest, the leaders of the group, Coxey and Carl Browne, were facing a tough choice. The group has started its march with much fanfare, leaving Massillon, Ohio, on Easter Sunday, March 25, and had since then made their way slowly eastward. The journey had thus far been tough on the men and they were averaging between 10 and 15 miles a day. To the east still lay many mountains to cross and just under two weeks to do it in.

May 1 was the designated date to be in Washington DC where Coxey would present his petition to Congress of his ideas for a national program of building and repairing roads that would also solve the national unemployment problem. Coxey's Army was a group of unemployed workers that had formed in Massillon. The official name of the group was the Commonweal of Christ, but most people referred to it as Coxey's Army.

Coxey decided to give his group a boost and he hired two C&O Canal boats to take the army to Williamsport. Tuesday morning, April 17, the group marched through Cumberland to the canal terminus and boarded the boats. "In the crowd was the Consolidated Coal Company freight agent; he had the unique job of deciding what should be the rental fare for the barges. After much calculation and many references to various rate books, he came up with a charge of $89 for Coxey's Army," wrote Grant.

The first boat was renamed "Good Roads" and was commanded by Coxey. It got underway around 12:30 p.m. "Sandy" Leitch supplied travel music on the bagpipes. The second boat, renamed "J.S. Coxey" got started about 20 minutes later. It was commanded by Carl Browne, the man the men had voted to lead them in Frostburg. On this boat, the Commonweal band played the travel music.

The reporters who were covering the event were forced to rent their own boat and follow the army down the canal to Williamsport.

From there, the group was able to meet their deadline date to get to Washington on foot where thousands of people lined the streets to watch them march through the city. However, things still did not go smoothly.

"Before the marchers could present their petition, the police rushed them, and Coxey and the other leaders were arrested for trampling on the grass," Scott wrote.

Though the group failed that day, what they sought to achieve resonated with the public. Fifty years later, Coxey was finally able to read his speech from the Capitol steps. Grant also notes that many of Coxey's ideas became part of President Franklin Delano Roosevelt's New Deal Programs.

A shorter version of this article appeared in the February/March 2008 issue of Allegany Magazine.

Mount Savage's "Merchant King" dies during surgery

On Monday evening, November 1, 1899, Mount Savage business-man R. H. Brannon closed up his shop on Main Street and headed home. While on his way home, he got caught in a rain shower and quickly took cold. However, the illness seemed to settle in his stomach and quickly plagued Brannon with painful stomach cramps.

Mount Savage physician Dr. Quarles made a house call and realized the seriousness of the illness. He called in Dr. Wiley and Dr. Johnson from Cumberland to consult on the case and see if they could offer Brannon relief. The Cumberland doctors decided that an operation would be needed and telegraphed for help from a specialist from Johns Hopkins Hospital in Baltimore.

The doctor arrived in the evening on Nov. 2. On Wednesday morn-ing, Nov. 3, the specialist began operating on Brannon for a bowel ob-struction. Unfortunately, Brannon died during the operation. He was only 45 years old.

"When the news of his death was received in this city a shock seemed to pervade the people, as no one was better known or better like than he," reported *The Evening Times* on Nov. 3.

Brannon was known as the "merchant king of Mt. Savage," accord-ing to the newspaper because of his successful general store at the cor-ner of Main Street and Water Street. "No man ever grew to prominence under more difficult circumstances or deserved more credit," according to *The Evening Times*.

R.H. BRANNON MEMORIAL BUILDING

R.H. Brannon, "Mount Savage's Merchant King," had a new store under construction in Mount Savage when he took sick on Nov. 1, 1899. He died two days later while undergoing surgery. Courtesy of the Mount Savage Historical Society.

Brannon had been orphaned at 10 years old and sent to live with his grandparents, Mr. and Mrs. Robert Harmon. Because his grandfather was blind, the young Brannon soon took the responsibility of supporting his grandparents on his own shoulders. His first job was in the foundry in town.

"Later in life he went into the huckstering business," reporter *The Evening Times*. "He rented a small room in Mt. Savage, where his hauled his produce and sold it."

That small business continued to grow into one of Mount Savage's largest businesses. In fact, a new, larger building was under construction to house his growing business when he died.

The newspaper noted that one reason Brannon would be missed was that, "unlike most successful business men, was charitable to a marked degree, and was of that disposition that made him everybody's friend and vice versa."

Besides being a business owner, he had also been Mount Savage's postmaster under President Grover Cleveland's administration. Brannon had also been a member and generous supporter of St. Patrick's Catholic Church in Mt. Savage.

This article appeared in the Cumberland Times-News on September 15, 2008.

Baltimore to Cumberland, the hard way

Nowadays, you can drive from Baltimore to Cumberland in two-and-half hours; less if you have a lead foot.

However, in 1901 automobile agent George Miller drove an automobile from the Baltimore to Cumberland for the first time. "The car was a 'one lung' Cadillac and it took him nearly two days to make the trip," reported the *Cumberland Evening Times* in 1922. A "one lung" automobile had only one cylinder.

Miller was the original agent in Baltimore for Waverley, Oldsmobile, Cadillac, Packard and Franklin automobiles.

"Everybody had it in for the auto those days. Speed limit was six miles per hour and the police took delight in arresting you. It took from one and a half to two days on a trip from Baltimore to Cumberland, simply because you had to stop, blindfold and lead around the machine every horse you met," Miller said in 1922.

The automobile industry was still in its infancy in 1901. This was still a year before the Ford Motor Company opened and the famous Model T didn't roll off the assembly line until 1908.

An 1899 issue of the *Hagerstown Mail* gave some perspective on the auto industry in America. That year, it was estimated that there were 15 million horses worth $500 million in the U.S. However, a New York firm had ordered $8 million in automobiles over two years and a million automobiles were expected to be built in 1900.

Martinsburg had only one car in it in 1899. It was sold at the end of the year meriting a short article in the *Hagerstown Mail* that noted, "The automobile will travel the streets of Martinsburg no more." Hagerstown also got its first automobile around the same time.

Miller also noted that on his trip from Baltimore to Cumberland that the automobile was still such a novelty that some people had never seen one and others were so scared of it that they ran and hid.

This 1901 Fiat, pictured on *www.wikimedia.com*, is one example of the type of car available to the public in that era.

While Miller handled many types of automobiles in Baltimore, there was one automobile actually made in Maryland at the time that he didn't handle and that was the steamer runabouts made by the Maryland Automobile Manufacturing Company in Luke. It was one of only four steam car manufacturers in the country at the time.

The Maryland Steamer was built from 1900-1901. It used a vertical two-cylinder steam engine and chain drive for power. The body was made of wood and it had large wooden-spoke wheels with solid rubber tires, according to *Maryland Automobile History*.

Only a few were built, but the Maryland Automobile Manufacturing also made variations on its design such as a racing car and delivery vans.

When Miller retired in 1922 and told the story of his journey from Baltimore to Cumberland, he was selling only Packards. His plan was to spend a lot of time driving around the country as an "auto bum." However, he made two predictions at the time. One was that trucks would overtake trains as the preferred way to transport freight on short trips within 10 years. Depending on how one defines a short trip, this was probably an accurate prediction.

His second prediction was that cheap, synthetic gas "will be on the market before long" distilled from plant and vegetable sources. While ethanol gas finally exists, I don't think anyone would argue that it is cheap.

This article appeared in the Cumberland Times-News on March 2, 2009.

A hidden fortune found in Cumberland home

Edward McKenna was known to those around him as a kind old man. He had emigrated from Ireland in his youth and made his home in Cumberland. He was a gardener who had a carefully tended vegetable garden in the backyard of his Fayette Street home near Saints Peter and Paul Church. He was especially known for his expertise in cultivating fruit trees, but given what was learned about him after he died, Edward McKenna would better remembered for his expertise in cultivating money trees.

When McKenna died on Feb. 8, 1905, he was 84 years old. Little note was made in the newspapers of his passing, just a few paragraphs on the obituary page that noted his love for gardening. His family and friends missed him, of course, and his wife was grief stricken, but McKenna was a man who had attracted little attention in his life.

He and his wife had lived a simple life. He made sure there was money to pay the bills and his wife made sure to spend their money wisely. All the while McKenna saved what he could for a rainy day that never came.

A week after McKenna's death, everyone wanted to know more about him. Not only were the local newspapers writing about Edward McKenna, but so were other regional newspapers.

The *Cumberland Alleganian* reported on Feb. 16, 1905, "Those who were well acquainted with Mr. McKenna knew he was a man of comfortable means and had a bank account, although from his practices of self denial and his continuing to labor and save one would be justified in believing he had barely the means to obtain the necessities for existence."

The Second National Bank at the corner of Baltimore and South Liberty streets was built in 1890. The building is now the home of Susquehanna Bank's main Cumberland Office. Courtesy of the Albert and Angela Feldstein Collection.

Indeed, even among those who knew him, many thought the McKennas were simply a kindly old couple living on a small income. Yet, following McKenna's funeral, $3,800 (nearly $100,000 in 2007 dollars) was found in the house he had shared with his 80-year-old wife. The money represented more than three years of income for a Cumberland family at that time. A single woman of Mrs. McKenna's age might be able to stretch that amount out for the rest of her life.

"The discovery was made by a neighbor, who was dusting the pictures at the McKenna home. The bulk of the money was in a large roll, although in bags suspended from nails behind the picture were considerable silver and gold coins. Money in smaller sums is said to have been found since Mr. McKenna's death in stockings, tin cans and the pockets of trousers," reported the *Emmitsburg Chronicle*.

The *Alleganian* also noted that the money was hidden in "valueless looking" packaging as if to hide it from any potential burglars, though reports said that is not a problem with which the McKennas had to deal.

Mrs. McKenna was so happy with the find that she immediately summoned a cab to take her to the Second National Bank at the corner of Baltimore and South Liberty streets in Cumberland.

As a side note, the Second National Bank, which was built in 1890, was designed by Cumberland native Bruce Price. "Price also happens to be the father of Emily Post of etiquette fame," wrote Al Feldstein in his book, *Feldstein's Top Historic Postcard Views of Allegany County, Maryland*. The building is now the home of Susquehanna Bank's main Cumberland office.

There she deposited the money and like a fairy tale, she lived happily ever after.

This article appeared in the Cumberland Times-News on August 7, 2007.

Mountain City residents
get first look
at the big screen

The Wonderland Theater had been in Frostburg for nearly 30 years; first as Paul's Hall and then Moat's Opera House. In that time, residents of the Mountain City had seen a lot of wonderful acts on the stage, but in 1907, they were about to see something new.

Paul's Hall was the second formal theater to open in Frostburg. It opened in 1876 just a few months after the Independent Order of Odd Fellows opened their performing hall. Before that time, performers in Frostburg used any large hall in town that would accommodate them.

Eventually, Paul's became Moat's Opera House. Then in 1907, James Davis remodeled Moat's and increased the seating to 400 and opened the Wonderland Theater. And with the remodel, Davis had also "installed a new Edison machine for projecting moving pictures, said to be finest outfit that money can buy," according to the February 2, 1907 *Frostburg Mining Journal*.

The state-of-the-art Edison projector at the time would have been the Universal Projecting Kinetoscope. They were lightweight machines that could be purchased as a complete outfit for $220 (about $5,000 today).

Moving pictures had been around for years using equipment such as the Thaumatrope or the Phenakistiscope. Thomas Edison invented the Kinetoscope in 1891. It had a motor for automated movement and the images were on film rather than paper.

Other improvement followed, including improvements Edison made to the Kinetoscope. It was in the early 1900's where both the projectors and the films reached a level that could be called movies.

In this famous scene from "The Great Train Robbery," 1903, one of the bandits fires his pistol at the audience. This scene scared viewers when the movie premiered, including those who enjoyed this first movie shown in Frostburg at the Wonderland Theater. Courtesy of www.legendsofamerica.com.

A writer for the *Frostburg Mining Journal* attended one of the showings of a movie at the Wonderland. Following the show, he wrote, "Clear and flickerless, it projects animated scenes with absolutely life like fidelity and astonishing realism. The scenes depicted before the eyes of the amazed auditor carry him quickly to foreign lands, strange places and historic localities. It is hard to believe that one views merely a reproduction of the startling events that appear before him. So natural they seem that one actually feels that he is viewing the incident itself."

Admission to the Wonderland cost five and 10 cents.

"The highlight of the first season was the showing of The Great

Train Robbery," wrote John Wiseman in *Allegany County-A History*.

The Great Train Robbery, filmed in 1903, is considered a movie milestone. It was a one-reel western that lasted only 10 minutes and had 14 scenes. It was filmed in Edison's New Jersey studio by Edwin S. Porter. The film was advertised as "a faithful duplication of the genuine 'Hold Ups' made famous by various outlaw bands in the far West." It was also based on a real-life 1900 train robbery by the "Hole in the Wall" Gang.

According to the Internet Movie Database, the movie's final shot of an outlaw firing a gun directly at the camera had such an effect on audiences that many of them thought they were actually about to be shot.

By April, the Wonderland was promoting special children's movies, such as Jack and the Beanstalk, another Edison picture.

Movies had caught on in Frostburg and the Wonderland had lived up to its name.

"In 1916, the Palace bought out the old Moat theater, changed its name to the Lyric, increased its seating to 700, and brought the year's most dramatic movie, The Birth of a Nation, to the Mountain City," Wiseman wrote.

This article appeared in the Cumberland Times-News on January 7, 2008.

Halloween a time for revelry

Oct. 31, 1907, began as most days did in Cumberland. People went to work. Children attended school. City work crews began paving Arch Street with bricks laid between Fourth and Fifth Streets. People shivered in the cold and moaned because frost was beginning to appear on the ground in the mornings.

Then the moon came up and the ghouls came out for Halloween 1907.

In South Cumberland, masked partiers gathered on Virginia Avenue, growing in number until about 9 p.m. when 600 people filled the streets and sidewalks. "About every second person was masked," reported the *Cumberland Evening Times*. The partiers crowded the street dancing, marching or wreaking a little good-natured havoc along Virginia Avenue. The noise and music was deafening but few people complained because they were having too much fun.

Three burlesque parades were going on at one time at different locations along the street. The participants wore ludicrous costumes and danced around in ridiculous twists and spins with arms and legs flopping about wildly. Young people threw corn, rice and confetti at the paraders who took the hits with a laugh and continued their gyrations. Later in the evening, every plate glass window on Virginia Avenue was soaped to a milky white by the partiers. The next morning, the *Cumberland Evening Times* reported, "a number of window glasses

Virginia Avenue, looking North, South Cumberland, Md.

217343

This is Virginia Avenue during the day around the time of this article, but on Halloween evening 1907, it took on quite a different look. Courtesy of Albert and the Angela Feldstein Collection.

were unusually clear this morning after their early baths."

A similar party was going on up and down Baltimore Street. "The men were dressed in costumes representing the opposite sex, while the latter tried to look like a man as if it were possible," the newspaper reported. While the streets of Cumberland had their share of revelers, many businesses and homes were just as crowded with private parties. Allegany Hospital on Decatur Street transformed its basement for the evening. As guests came down the stairs to the basement, they entered a room decorated with fall leaves, cornstalks, pumpkins and hay bales. Two female ghosts greeted the guests and guided them to a long white corridor that glowed eerily in a feeble light created by alcohol burning in pans of sand. At the end of the corridor, the guests entered a red tent. Wanda the fortuneteller sat behind a table reading the fortunes of those who approached. She laid out the rows of Tarot cards and stared at the characters and saw good fortune in the guests' futures. She pointed the guest to the tent's exit and they entered the front room where there was plenty of room for dancing to the live music from Albert Himmler on violin and Samuel Landis on guitar. In a rear room, the guests played party games and ate their suppers.

Elsewhere in town, the Queen City Skating Rink was crowded with about 1,000 "ghosts, goblins, witches and many others held sway," reported the newspaper. About 100 of them took part in a grand parade around the rink.

At the Potomac Club, autumn leaves, cornstalks and pumpkins decorated the building for a masquerade dance followed by a dinner. Students and faculty at the Allegany Academy on Washington Street had their own masquerade party.

Individuals had parties like the one held in the home of L.D. Rohrer on Baltimore Street. Rohrer's grandson G.L. Rohrer gave the party in the home "decorated in a ghost-like manner and goblins were seated all around." The supper featured pumpkin pie and apple cider. Russell Bortz, Ray Wilson, Henrietta Twigg, Adelaide Spicer, Cecelia Richard, George Rohrer, James Cable, Ralph Morgart, Paul Miller, Georgia Belt, Samuel Weiskettle were some of the ghosts and goblins in attendance.

The next morning was Friday. People went to work. Children attended school. City work crews continued paving Arch Street. People complained because frost was on the ground. But they smiled when they recalled the night before and laughed when they told each other their stories from Halloween 1907.

This article appeared in the Cumberland Times-News on June 28, 2004.

Police officer mortally wounded in Shantytown

There's no harm in a drink once in a while or so the saying goes, but those harmless little drinks once cost two men their lives, nearly ruined a hospital, nearly killed one man and got another man beaten up. Not that unusual for an evening in Shantytown.

William Burns and Jesse Page were winding down from their workdays on Thursday, Oct. 4, 1907. They headed down to Wineow Street in the Shantytown section of Cumberland. They stopped in Kate Preston's Saloon and ordered themselves drinks. It wasn't long before both men were a bit tipsy. Jesse's attention was pulled to another area of the bar and he wandered away from William.

No one would later remember how the argument began but it ended with William getting into a fight with another person at the bar. The fight continued outside of the bar on the pavement.

The fight caught the attention of Cumberland Police Officer August Baker, who was walking his beat along Wineow Street.

Baker broke up the fight but William was still belligerent and trying to fight. Baker decided to arrest him but William resisted arrest. James Hussey, a bartender at J.M. Fields Saloon was in the doorway watching the fight, which had ended up outside of his doors. He reported that Baker raised his club and threatened to hit William if he did not go along to the station peacefully. William pulled a revolver and shot Baker about an inch below his heart.

"You dirty dog. You shot me," Baker said. Despite his wound,

Baker still managed to club and handcuff William before he passed out.

Humphrey Green, a bystander, stood over William, making sure he didn't run away until Officer John Trieber arrived. Robert King and Officer O'Neill rushed Baker to the Baltimore Street entrance of the Western Maryland Hospital.

O'Neill told Nurse Kenney about the incident and asked for a stretcher to bring in Baker. Kenney told him that there was one in the hallway he could use. She called the hospital superintendent who told her to call in a surgeon and get the operating room ready. When she went back to see Baker and admit him, he was gone.

O'Neill had only seen a wheelchair in the hallway, which could not have gotten Baker up the stairs and into the hospital. Faced with that, O'Neill and King took Baker to Allegany Hospital where he was admitted. Baker was operated on but the outlook was not good.

By 8 p.m. Friday night, his pulse was weak and his breathing heavy. By midnight, he had lapsed into a coma which he came out of only once briefly. *The Cumberland Daily News* reported, "During that brief period of consciousness he complained of fearful agony. By his side was his faithful wife, although during the last few hours he was unconscious of her presence."

He died about 3:30 a.m. on Saturday morning. His funeral was held Monday afternoon and presided over by Rev. C. F. Floto of St. Stephen's Lutheran Church. Baker was buried in Greenmont Cemetery.

On Wednesday, the Cumberland Mayor and City Council launched an inquiry into the management of Western Maryland Hospital "in consequence of a seeming manifestation of unconcern, lack of facilities or possible failure to conform with certain red tape regulation promulgated by the management, those ministering to the dying officer felt compelled to go elsewhere," reported the newspaper.

The hospital was eventually cleared of any negligence. Jesse surrendered himself to police and was nearly lynched alongside William, but it is what happened to William that became the shame of Cumberland.

Cumberland Police Officer August Baker's beat included the Shantytown area of the city. It was here that he was fatally shot by William Burns in 1907. Courtesy of the Cumberland City Council from the Herman and Stacia Miller Collection.

Citizens take law into their own hands

A police officer was dead but his murderer had been caught and put in jail. That wasn't enough for some people. They wanted an eye for an eye. Blood for blood. A life for a life. William Burns shot Cumberland Police Officer August Baker in Shantytown on Thursday, Oct. 4, 1907. Baker died early Saturday morning at Allegany Hospital.

His death started people talking about making sure the murderer met his maker. The *Cumberland Daily News* reported, "It was not given credence in public circles, upon the presumption that as there had never been a lynching in Cumberland." Never say never.

On Saturday around 10:30 p.m., men came in twos and threes and gathered at the intersection of Johnson and Greene streets at the base of the hill below the jail. Lookouts were posted on Prospect Square to make sure there were no police nearby.

Deputy Sheriff Noah Hendley heard a rap at the door of the jail. He looked out an upstairs window and saw a mob of about 200 men filling the street in front of the jail.

"Come down and open the door," someone called. Hendley knew a mob when he saw one and he knew they were up to no good.

"I will do nothing of the kind and I will shoot the first man who steps inside the door," he said.

"Batter down the door," people in the mob began to call.

About 50 men rushed down the hill to Greene Street where a telegraph pole lay. They hefted it onto their shoulders and carried it up the steep incline. They rammed the pole against the wooden doors of the jail.

From inside, Hendley aimed his pistol at the door and pleaded with them to let the law take its course. Amid cheers and hand clapping, the wooden double doors splintered. The mob surged inside. Hendley was overpowered and disarmed. The mob tore at his clothing and threatened his life.

The mob tried to use the pole to open the steel corridor doors open that led to the prisoner's exercise room. Unlike the front doors, these doors held. The mobbers searched Hendley and found the keys to open the door. They searched every cell looking for Burns. Frightened inmates obliged them and pointed out that Burns' cell was the last cell on the right hand side of the corridor. They mobbers choked the narrow corridor. They fought to pry open the old lock but it held. After 10 minutes, they gave up and used the telegraph pole to hammer it open.

Inside the cell, Burns cowered speechlessly in the shadows of his cell. The mobbers grabbed him and carried him along toward the outer doors. When he resisted, he was punched. When he fell, he was dragged, first head first and then feet first down the steps of the jail to the cobbled street.

As the mob emptied from the jail, Hendley went back to see the damage and if anyone else had been hurt. What he found was that the 26 prisoners were slowly being asphyxiated.

In the mob's eagerness to batter down the door to Burn's cell, they had also broken the gas pipes in the room. Hendley sealed them as best he could and then opened all of the windows in the jail to ventilate the room.

Outside, the Rev. William Cleveland Hicks from Emmanuel Episcopal Church had heard the tumult and came to see what was happening. Dressed in his cassock, he stood on the jail steps with his hands held high, pleading with the men to obey the law of God and man and disperse.

"The mob had apparently provided no rope as when it was suggested that the body be dragged to the West Virginia bridge and strung up, no hemp was forthcoming," reported the newspaper.

The mobbers kicked at Burns and tore at his clothing. Then a shot rang out, quickly followed by at least a dozen more. "The men who fired the bullets stood right in the glare of the electric light, one alone firing the contents of a seven-shooter into the fallen form of Burns," reported the newspaper.

Some of the mobbers had masked their faces with handkerchiefs, other blackened their faces, but many made no attempt at concealment.

Even after Burns lay dead, the mobbers continued to kick him and shoot him. "Burn him! Burn him!" some of the mobbers cried. Matches were struck and the search for flammable material began.

Hicks pleaded for the mob not to violate the body anymore. "The deed done, the mob seemed to listen to Rev. Hicks' plea for mercy and many began to edge away from the scene," reported the *Cumberland Daily News.*

Judge Hunter Boyd arrived on the scene shortly after Hicks. Seeing some response to Hicks' plea, Boyd moved to the center of the crowd and launched into a speech condemning the mob's actions. At the conclusion of his speech the mob applauded him and hundreds began to withdraw from the scene.

"While the lynching was in progress and the mob was forcing entrance into the jail, Mr. B.A. Richmond and a number of citizens endeavored to get the police to the jail, but as they were scattered all over the city, from the Narrows to Virginia Lane patrolling their beats, it was fully an hour before the first squad arrived, long after the mob had done its awful work and the blood-smeared form of the dead Negro lay in the street directly opposite the jail doors," reported the newspaper.

Louis Stein, the undertaker, arrived soon after the police, but it took another hour before he was able to get help to load the body and take it away to his funeral home. Spectators and curiosity seekers took pieces of Burns' clothing and blood-covered stones as mementos of the event.

Later, a crowd of 10,000 people, including Sunday school children, paraded through Stein's funeral home to see the body. Boyd asked for an investigation of the lynching Tuesday.

He told the grand jury, "I say that anyone connected with that occurrence was guilty of murder and nothing else but murder.When Officer Baker had received a mortal wound, what did he do? He turned the man over to officers of the law. Officer Baker's memory has been insulted. Officer Baker was fearless, brave and upright. Yet he wanted the law to take its course and the mob's action was a reflection upon the good officer's memory. The action of the mob was contrary to practice of the law."

The county commissioners offered a $500 reward for information leading to the arrest and convictions of any of the mobbers, but no one ever came forward. "It is said that some of the lynchers are known and that the mob included several prominent citizens who have never been known to carry revolvers, but who did so upon this occasion," reported the newspaper.

At first it appeared Burns would be buried in a pauper's grave, but his sister eventually came to Cumberland from Pittsburgh to claim the body of the victim of Cumberland's only lynching.

These articles appeared in the Cumberland Times-News on August 16 and 17, 2004.

City was a "Paragon" of the auto industry

There was a time when Motor City was going to be just that, a city of motors without the cars.

In 1918, cars were becoming more and more popular across the country. Automobile manufacturing was a growth industry and many people were looking to become part of the manufacturing boom. Cumberland already had a piece of the pie with Kelly-Springfield Tire Co. headquarters.

Then in April, the Paragon Motor Co. Board of Directors unanimously voted to change the proposed location of its plant from Connellsville, Pa., to Cumberland. The company opened offices in the J.P. Wiesel Building on Baltimore Street.

The board called Cumberland "one of the most-aggressive and wide-awake small cities in the United States" and "Cumberland, as an industrial center is, we find, admirably situated for the manufacture of Paragon Motor Cars..."

The site for the plant was 20 acres near the current Motor City. The plan was to construct a $3 million plant that would employ 600 people and manufacture motors for the new line of cars. Paragon expected to produce about 500 cars a year.

That month the *Cumberland Evening Times*, "Motor experts have pronounced the motor one of the most powerful and efficient in their knowledge."

Though Paragon intended to manufacture four cars, three prototypes were built. There was a two-passenger roadster, a two-passenger
with a yacht deck (similar to a pickup truck) and a five-passenger se-
dan. They would sell for between $3,000 and $3,500, depending on the
model. As Paragon officials toured potential building sites around the
area, they drove the prototypes to advertise the future of motor cars.

Once the announcement was made, the company began selling
stock among local residents who were excited to be part of the new
venture. The one cautionary point was that although Paragon President
Philip Blake was secretary of the Chamber of Commerce, the chamber
withheld its support of the project. Because of his involvement with
the company, Blake was asked to resign his position in June and did
so.

In July, the chamber researched the idea and reported favorably on
the mechanical design, construction and performance of the Paragon
cars. Executive Committee Chairman Henry Shriver wrote, "The Paragon Motor Car Co. has a very excellent car which will compare favorably with other well-known makes that have an established reputation
throughout the country."

The problem was with the company's finances. The chamber noted
that some information wasn't forthcoming and what was available
suggested that Paragon would need to sell far too much stock in order
to generate its needed working capital.

Despite the failure of the chamber to support the project, the cornerstone was laid on Mount Savage Road on Aug. 28. The day's
events began with a dance at 2:30 p.m. and the cornerstone ceremony
at 4 p.m.

Cumberland Mayor Thomas Koon gave the opening remarks wel-
coming the beginning of a new industry in the area. Chamber President
William Sperry poured the concrete for the first pier of the new building.

Thomas Pownell spoke at the ceremony. He said, "Our slogan is
Build a Paragon here at Cumberland. ... Build one as good as the Ford
and at Ford prices, and Henry Ford, the greatest motor man in all the
world, will congratulate you, and the usefulness of the Paragon will be
known from shore to shore."

He also said something that would become prophetic in how highly
inaccurate it turned out to be, "I am glad, gentlemen, that booming and

boasting (about the company) are absent, which omens that busting will be absent."

But a bust is actually what the entire project turned out to be.

In February and March of 1922, the chamber was running newspaper notices warning people about the dangers of fake stock-selling schemes.

In March, the chamber responded to a letter from Mrs. Wise, reminding her that the chamber hadn't endorsed the Paragon project. While she had not received her Paragon stock, the chamber told her there was little to be done except to contact the bank that issued the stock. The chamber also noted it had warned Paragon not to try and collect people who had backed out of stock purchases, because the chamber would defend them.

Cumberland's chance to rival Detroit evaporated with crushed and costly dreams.

This article appeared in the Cumberland Times-News on March 17, 2004.

Ridgeley is an example of what a vote means

When J.T. Bowers walked into Baker's Barber Shop in Ridgeley, West Virginia, it wasn't for a shave and a haircut. He wanted to vote in the 1914 elections, just like he expected most everyone on Ridgeley was doing that Thursday. What J.T. didn't realize was that his vote would change the future of the small town on the banks of the Potomac River.

The question had been talked about for a year, "Should Ridgeley incorporate and become a town?" Every one of Ridgeley's 1,300 residents seemed to have an opinion and J.T., who had moved to Ridgeley in October 1913 and lived there since then (except for three months when he had been forced to live temporarily in Cumberland), was no different.

In anticipation of a big voter turnout, the polls had opened at 6:45 a.m. J.T. didn't see much of a line when he went to vote shortly before 6 p.m. The polls would be open for another hour, which is when a majority of the voters, who were employed by the Western Maryland Railroad and didn't get off work until 5:30 p.m., were expected to cast their ballots.

The *Cumberland Evening Times* reported that 135 votes had been cast by 3 p.m. and those in favor of incorporation were claiming a 20-vote lead at that point.

While 135 votes might seem a small number of votes in town of 1,300, only 237 men were registered voters. In the years before the

19th Amendment was added to U.S. Constitution in 1920, only men could vote. So it while everyone would be affected by the outcome of the vote, it was the men of Ridgeley who would decide the town's future.

The voting district of which Ridgeley was a part of a voting district that had seen the number of registered voters increase from 343 in the 1912 election to 407 for the 1914 election and The *Cumberland Evening Times* noted, "The increase is in Ridgeley alone as there is scarce if any increase in the rural district."

Yet, there was one man in Ridgeley who was wanted to vote but wasn't allowed although he was registered. That was J.T.

The election judge told him that because he had left Ridgeley for three months earlier in the year, he wasn't eligible to vote in Ridgeley's election now. It didn't matter that J.T. hadn't wanted to move. He'd had to because the house he had been renting in Ridgeley had been sold. He hadn't been able to find a new place to live in a reasonable time so he'd been forced to move across the river to Cumberland. He hadn't stopped looking for a place in live in Ridgeley, though, and had been able to move back in August.

But the election judge said he hadn't lived in Ridgeley long enough so his vote didn't count.

The truth was very much the opposite. That vote would count very much.

Ridgeley's roots date back to when the early Americans looked west. Eastern seaboard planters founded the Ohio Company in 1748 to develop the fur trade through the Allegheny Mountains. The company then built a small storehouse on the south side of the Potomac River in 1750. "The building was stoutly constructed, and was large enough so that it not only provided space for the accommodation of trade goods and precious furs, but also served as the residence of the agent and his family," wrote Gordon Kershaw in *Allegany County-A History*. The Ohio Company agents could be considered as the first residents of what would become Ridgeley, West Virginia, though it was neither at the time.

Because of its stout construction, the storehouse served as a defensive location and was eventually referred to as Fort Ohio. It was considered the northernmost in a chain of forts that helped protect settlers during the French and Indian War. "Ft Ohio stocked 4000 (English Pounds) worth of merchandise purchased in London for the Indian trade in the Ohio," wrote Mary Riggleman Frye in her manuscript *History of Ridgeley, West Virginia.*

In the early 1800s, the Charles Ridgeley family settled in the area and the Ridgeley built their home on the banks of the river and across the street from the present Ridgeley Town Hall. Charles made the bricks for the home in his own brickyard and used stones from the Potomac to form the foundation.

According to Frye, the town, or at least a part of it, was originally named St. Clarisville. "It was given the name because of a donation of 10 acres of land to the county seat by a man named St. Clair, to encourage erection of the Blue Bridge crossing the Potomac River from Allegany County, Md.," she wrote.

Later, John P. Barncord opened the first grocery store in the town and was also in charge of the post office, calling the address "Barncord, W.Va." "Thus we had two towns, St. Clarisville and Barncord, and a flag station at Ridgeley - which was very confusing to the public," wrote Frye. R.A. Radcliffe was appointed postmaster in 1898 and named the town after the Ridgeley family.

As Ridgeley grew, residents found themselves sorely in need of things that the county government couldn't afford to give the town, such as better lighting, more police protection and sewers. The way for the town to get these things was to incorporate and charge a municipal tax to residents. "It is the only way in which the people can have what they have so badly needed for some time that is lights, protections, walks and sewerage, which will come in the course of a few years," reported *The Cumberland Evening Times* in 1914.

Incorporation became the hot topic for the town and both sides were out trying to persuade voters to see things their way. On Oct. 2, a public meeting was held in the school. Keyser attorney W.C. Grimes and Mineral County Sheriff Nethkin attended the meeting and spoke in favor of incorporation. "It was clearly shown at the meeting that many were in favor of the progressive move of the town; it was also evident that there were some against it. It seems however that as the time for deciding the question is at hand those in favor of the question are in the majority," reported the *Cumberland Evening Times.*

Opposition came from people who said the rents of the houses would go up $6 to $12 a year if the town was incorporated. Those in favor said that municipal taxes wouldn't increase rents by that much and would be offset by elimination of the county roads tax and the district road levy. Fire insurance rates would also be lower in an incorporated town.

Most people seemed to think that incorporation would pass easily. At the end of election day, October 15, 1914, 210 men, or 89 percent of the registered voters in town had voted.

The final tally was 105 for incorporation and 105 against.

J.T. knew he had to take action. If he had been allowed to vote the decision wouldn't have been a tie. R.A. Radcliffe, William Everstine, C.A. Jewell, Ferman H. Moreland, H.E. Valentine and G.W. Spangler petitioned the Mineral County Circuit Court to allow J.T.'s vote to count. J.T.'s lawyer argued, "During the time that Mr. Bowers lived in Cumberland, he never gave up his claim to a vote in Ridgeley as he only was in Cumberland until he could get back in Ridgeley," reported The Cumberland Evening Times.

Judge F.M. Reynolds ruled that the vote would count Nov. 28 and Ridgeley was allowed to incorporate. The search then began for candidates to be the founding fathers of Ridgeley. Among the candidates for mayor and town councilmen were a full slate put forth by the Socialist Party. The first election was held January 7, 1915 and James T. Vandergrift became the first mayor of Ridgeley.

The *Cumberland Evening Times* summed up the importance of incorporation for the town, reporting after a stretch of rain in December 1914, "For the last week or so no one would think to go over the streets of Ridgeley that they had suddenly dropped into some of the side streets of Venice and a small boat would be quite a help in traversing from place to place. So much is needed in the way of general improvement for the town that it is rather hard to say which is most important. One thing, however, and that is lights with proper police protection, seems to be the general cry from all parts of town. Little by little with the same well done, and not to over do anything, will eventually accomplish much for the town."

The town is smaller now as are most places in the region that have suffered from the exodus of industry in the middle of the last century. Ridgeley, according to the U.S. Census, has a little over 700 people, but it still has a mayor and town council and it can still provide its citizens with the services they need.

The town structure helped residents recover from floods in 1924, 1936 and 1937 that put most of the buildings in town under water. The

1936 flood, in particular, sent eight feet of water down the streets of town and displaced 1,200 people for two days.

Never let it be said that your vote doesn't make a difference. One vote created Ridgeley.

A shorter version of this article appeared in the Cumberland Times-News on September 20, 2004.

Got milk? Get killed.

During the late summer of 1915, Cumberland was plagued with a serial killer stalking the city's children. Within two weeks at the beginning of September, eight small children in Cumberland died in pain.

The killer: milk.

"These deaths are usually due to lack of care and lack of proper food. Children who do not have to rely upon cow's milk as their means of sustaining life are very fortunate, but those who must either use cow's milk or some other substitute that is not even as good, must suffer the consequence whenever the milk is in such shape that is not fit for their use," City Health Officer Max Colton told the *Cumberland Evening Times* in September 1915.

The children were dying from a disease known as "Summer Complaint." It began with milk that was either unpasteurized or allowed to get too warm, which allowed bacteria to grow in the milk.

Summer Complaint attacked children between two months and three years old. It occurred during warm weather and primarily in cities like Cumberland. And it was often fatal. The symptoms were profuse diarrhea and an inability for the child to keep anything down. The child would then develop fever, thirst and delirium. If the child's immune system wasn't strong enough, he or she would die.

"The only way in which children can be safe-guarded against this disease is through clean milk and where such is not obtainable mothers should pasteurize the milk in their own homes. Commercially pasteurized milk, unless properly conducted, is not much better than the original raw milk as is sold on the market. This department will welcome any questions from any mothers who desire to know the condition of their dealer's milk. It must be born in mind by mothers that when milk is received in the home, proper care must be given it in order that it will not become any worse than what it actually is when left at the door," Colton said.

Before dairies started using refrigerated trucks to deliver milk, like in this early shot of the Queen City Dairy, milk could breed bacteria that would sicken children. Courtesy of the Albert and Angela Feldstein Collection.

Milkmen delivered bottled milk directly to homes durin g this time in history. The milk men kept the milk cold in wagons cooled by ice. If no one was home when the milkman came to deliver the milk, he simply left it in a box by the door. If the milk wasn't kept cool, there was a chance for bacteria to breed even in pasteurized milk.

Whether Colton's warning helped save any lives is unknown because as the weather began to turn colder, it was easier to keep the milk refrigerated even when left outside.

LOOKING BACK

Summer Complaint deaths continued to be a problem for decades until the causes were better understood and better ways to transport and store milk came about with electric refrigeration.

This article appeared in the Cumberland Times-News on May 11, 2009.

Queen City leaders brought up on bribery charges in scandal of 1914

Sheriff Harry Irvine felt uncomfortable as he watched the suspect walking. Something about this felt wrong or maybe it was simply because he knew the man he now had to arrest. Irvine walked up to Ward Eichelberger as he paused at the intersection of Harrison and South Mechanic Streets in Cumberland. Eichelberger saw the sheriff and greeted him.

"Ward, you're under arrest," Irvine said quickly getting to the point. Eichelberger's smile fell and his shoulders drooped. "I know that I am in bad," he said, according to the *Cumberland Evening Times*. "I did wrong, but did not get any of the money. Hummelshine did it all."

A short time later Theodore Hummelshine and his son, Bruce, were also arrested.

The next afternoon Cumberland residents read in the *Cumberland Evening Times* of September 23, 1914: "BRIBERY CHARGE AGAINST OFFICIALS."

Theodore Hummelshine was the Cumberland police and fire commissioner and Eichelberger was the finance commissioner. They had been charged with soliciting a bribe. Bruce Hummelshine had been charged with conspiracy.

The alleged bribe centered on $8,000 owed the New York contractor, Merrill, Ruckgaber and Company for work on the Evitt's Creek

Water System. Detective Elmer Miller had caught the commissioners in a sting operation. The newspaper reported "the accused Commissioners entered into an agreement with Miller, who claimed to be a member or representative of Merrill, Ruckgaber and Company, to procure payment of the $8,000, claimed to be due the contractors, in consideration of the payment of $800 to them."

The commissioners were each released on $5,000 bail and they continued to serve in their city positions as they awaited trial. It was not an easy time for either man.

Theodore Hummelshine responded in the Nov. 13 Cumberland Press to Mayor Thomas Koons' public comments. Hummelshine considered the comments a "violent attack upon me, as head of the Police Department, by the Mayor of the City."

Hummelshine further said, "I wish to say to the mayor that I have a clear conscience both as to my public and private record in Cumberland, and that when he attacks me, he attacks one who can and will defend himself to the fullest extent."

The defense claimed that the Cumberland businessmen who hired Miller had tried to frame the commissioners. Hummelshine and Eichelberger claimed they had actually been trying to uncover the bribery plot and trap a crooked contractor. They said States Attorney Frank Perdew knew of their efforts and would be testifying on their behalf at the trial.

The trial began Nov. 11 in a crowded courtroom. F. Brooke Whiting, George Louis Eppler and Arch Young were the defense lawyers and Albert Doub was prosecuting in place of Perdew, who had recused himself from the case because he was a defense witness.

Doub's opening statements took an hour. He promised to show the jury conversations between Hummelshine and Miller that had been recorded on an extension phone, Eichelberger's incriminating statement and that Theodore Hummelshine had been present when his son accepted $100 from John W. George "to use his influence in having the Green Ridge Ku-Klux case against John W. George come to nothing," according to the newspaper report.

During Whiting's opening statements, he laid out the conspiracy, saying that a lawyer involved with the case had said, "You may elect Dr. Hummelshine to the council, but I will send him to the penitentiary if you do."

In the second day of testimony, one of the transcribed conversations was introduced as evidence. Theodore Hummelshine and Miller had spoken by phone about when Hummelshine could get the approval for the city to pay off the overdue bill passed. A stenographer sat next to an extension phone in another room of Miller's office and recorded the conversation this way:

Miller: And when can this thing be put through?

Hummelshine: Leave that to me.

Miller: Can it be put through next week?

Hummelshine: Yes.

Miller: This is final now.

Hummelshine: Goodbye.

Whiting tried to discredit the phone conversations by saying that the C&P Telephone Company may have been a part of the conspiracy because Hummelshine was against the merger of C&P and the Western Maryland Telephone Company.

After a second day of testimony, both sides rested their cases. The jury deliberated for only an hour and came back with a guilty verdict. "A large crowd had lingered at the courthouse to hear the verdict, which came as a great surprise, for the impression held by the great number who had heard the testimony was that the verdict would be that of acquittal," the *Cumberland Evening Times* reported.

The defendants filed a motion for a new trial, which was turned down. The two councilmen were fined $200 each and sentenced to three months in prison and Bruce Hummelshine was fined $100 and two months in prison.

Though both men had to leave their city offices, Hummelshine was re-elected as the commissioner of police and fire in 1918 and served until his death 1921.

This article appeared in the Cumberland Times-News on April 2, 2007.

Millions "died struggling" with Spanish Flu

The Spanish Flu began with a cough and muscle aches. It ended in death. Not in every case, but forty million of them ended that way.

In 1918, the world was at war with a deadly enemy. The two battled for about a year until the enemy retreated and hid but not before killing about forty million people or more than seven times the population of Maryland.

It was not World War I that killed all those people. It was the Spanish Flu. It was called Spanish Flu because its first noted appearance was in Spain, but it was simply 1918's flu strain, a strain that happened to be deadly.

The problem with the flu virus is that it mutates fairly easily and you are never sure of how virulent a flu you will wind up with. The SARS scare killed a few hundred people out of a worldwide population of four billion plus. Now imagine the terror people felt in 1918 about a flu that killed two-hundred-thousand times the number killed by SARS in a world that was half as populated.

Spanish Flu killed more people than were killed in World War I and in a shorter time frame, too, yet the war captured the headlines during 1918. Estimates are six-hundred-and-seventy-five-thousand Americans died from the Spanish Flu or ten times more than died in the war.

People had reason to fear for their lives.

Spanish Flu killed more people in one year than the Black Plague did in four years.

Spanish Flu was so devastating that human life span was reduced by ten years in 1918.

After one month in Philadelphia, the flu had killed nearly eleven thousand people, including almost eight hundred people on October 10, 1918.

The Lloyd Lowndes house at the corner of Washington Street and Prospect Square served as an emergency hospital for up to 100 patients during the Spanish Flu pandemic in 1918. The home has since been razed. Courtesy of the Albert and Angela Feldstein Collection.

One physician wrote that patients rapidly "develop the most vicious type of pneumonia that has ever been seen" and later when cyanosis appeared in patients "it is simply a struggle for air until they suffocate." Another doctor said that the influenza patients "died struggling to clear their airways of a blood-tinged froth that sometimes gushed from their mouth and nose."

The reactions at the time were sometimes draconian. Washington, D.C. passed a law that it was illegal to appear outdoors. San Francisco and San Diego forced their citizens to wear gauze masks. Some towns required a signed certificate if someone wanted to enter the town.

In Allegany County, the *Cumberland Evening Times* took little notice of the flu until the end of September. At that time, the article was about the effect of the flu on other places and the problems it was causing.

Then people began to get sick and die in Allegany County.

On October 4, 1918, the Board of Health passed an order closing schools, churches, theaters and dance halls. Streetcars and other public transportation had to travel with windows open. Plus, a person couldn't spit on the street and needed to use a handkerchief when he or she coughed or sneezed. This is because fresh air was believed to be the best defense against Spanish Flu. County Commissioner James McAlpine was the interim health officer at the time and Ralph Rizer signed the order.

The order came too late to help much. All of the obituaries for people who died the day the Board of Health's order was issued died from Spanish Influenza. The same issue of the paper also noted that hospitals were so helpless about treating the flu, they didn't want to risk spreading the flu to other patients who would be susceptible. They asked that flu cases not be brought to the hospitals.

How bad was the flu in Allegany County? The Baltimore and Ohio Railroad had six thousand employees in the county at that time; one thousand of them reported sick with the flu on October 4.

One of the problems with combating the flu was that modern medicine was still in its infancy. People just didn't know much about germ theory let alone viruses, which are even smaller. No real defense or treatment for the flu existed.

Doctors developed crude vaccines or throat gargles by straining blood and mucus from people who had survived the flu. The vaccines were injected into people's arms. The gargles were sprayed in a person's throat. Both had no effect.

On October 5, pool halls and bars were added to the places the Board of Health closed during the epidemic. Drug clerks were becoming overworked trying to fill all of the orders for medicines. They weren't the only ones, either.

One article in the *Cumberland Evening Times* said, "The physicians of the city are having a hard time trying to do justice to their many patients. Three prominent physicians are confined to their homes with the prevailing ailment, hence their patients have to be looked after by other doctors, and the shortage of physicians makes it all the harder for those who are able to make the rounds and also to respond to new calls constantly coming in.

"The department stores, in fact the stores generally, are all hard pushed for help. At one large department store it was stated this morning that they were short some thirty-two clerks."

The doctor problem was one of the insidious ways Spanish Flu worked. It not only sickened a person, requiring them to need medical attention, but it sickened doctors and nurses making them unavailable to treat patients who desperately needed their help.

The *Cumberland Evening Times* wrote, "The number of cases up to and including yesterday which have come under the notice of the physicians total four thousand. This, of course, does not include the cases which have not been attended by any doctors, which would increase the number to a large extent."

On October 7, the city hospitals, Western Maryland (Memorial) and Allegany (Sacred Heart), were afraid to admit flu patients because it might spread to the other patients.

An emergency hospital operated by the Red Cross was opened on the Sprigg property on 28 Washington Street that was owned by the Lowndes family. James W. Thomas who owned the property across the street donated it to serve as a nurses' residence. The hospital was expected to accommodate one hundred patients.

Since the schools were closed because of the Board of Health order, the board of education asked the teachers to volunteer at the hospitals.

Churches like St. Patrick's and Saints Peter and Paul held their services outside to comply with the health order.

The Central YMCA offered its public areas as an emergency hospital.

The physicians created a ward system throughout the city to try and handle the demand for treatment with thinning resources.

By October 8, people began to realize the problem was even worse than the Board of Health thought. First off, influenza was not a disease doctors had to report. It became one after this epidemic. Second, because the doctors were short handed, they weren't filling out the death reports that they should have been. This led to an under reporting of deaths attributable to the flu.

As the number of deaths increased, the shortage extended to grave-diggers. The *Cumberland Evening Times* reported, "Several funerals may have to be postponed because grave diggers at Rose Hill cemetery are overtaxed. It was reported this afternoon that orders were in for ten graves to be dug, but one so far had been prepared."

An article in the *Journal of the Alleghenies* read, "Bodies of Frostburg servicemen stationed at Fort Meade were sent back to Frostburg wrapped in blankets and tagged. Their bodies were stored temporarily in the corner house where the Frostburg Legion building now stands. Behind the post office in a carriage house, open doors revealed bodies laid on the floor. At the Durst Funeral Home from October 5 to October 31, 1919, ninety-nine bodies were prepared for the last rites. Those bodies, placed in rough caskets or wooden boxes, were carted to the cemetery and stacked until burial."

The phone company also pleaded for people to only utilize the phones in case of emergency because they were short operators because of the flu.

On October 9, the *Cumberland Evening Times* reported, "It is said that the deaths being recorded are greater than at any other time in the history of the town unless it was in Civil War days when there was a cholera epidemic."

It was also reported in the newspaper that nurses were being overworked. "The hospitals are seriously handicapped in handling cases because so many nurses being ill from influenza. At the Western Maryland, it was stated thirteen nurses were incapacitated and all but three were able to look after patients. At the Allegany Hospital, the situation is almost identical, the nurses who are able to be on duty being worked to the limit."

Things worsened. Twelve people died in one day in Lonaconing. Arrests were made because streetcars traveled with their windows closed.

Coal production in the numerous mines in the George's Creek region fell off because the miners took sick.

The size and colors of wreaths hung on doors of homes indicated who had died in the house.

Some help came with special trains sponsored by the state and federal governments that were traveling hospitals. Emergency hospitals were opened at the B&O YMCA on Virginia Avenue and Laughlin's Hall in Piedmont.

At this point, the B&O Railroad, which had one-thousand workers out earlier now had thirty-five-hundred people – nearly six out of every ten railroad workers in Cumberland – out sick with the flu.

Finally, by October 16, doctors began to report that they were catching up in their case loads. Over the next couple weeks, new cases began to drop off and the hospitals began to empty of flu patients. On October 25, the Board of Health ban was finally lifted.

Because of the problems with reporting, the precise number of Allegany County residents who died from Spanish Influenza is only a range. It appears that four hundred to five hundred residents died of the Spanish Flu during October. That is equivalent to losing a town the size of Barton or Midland in one month.

It is the deadliest plague that has ever struck the world and yet, it remains largely forgotten either through the selective memories of the people who lived through it or because history books remember World War I and not the flu.

Whatever the reason, October 1918 remains the month that the world mourned.

A shorter version of this article appeared in the Cumberland Times-News on April 12, 2004.

Cumberland's first councilwoman would not serve

Cumberland's Police and Fire Commissioner T.A.K. Hummelshine had been dead for two weeks. It had come as a surprise to no one when he succumbed to a "creeping paralysis" on May 9, 1921. To attend his final council meetings, he had needed someone to carry him to the meeting room.

But Hummelshine was buried, and now the responsibility to find his replacement fell upon Mayor Thomas Koon and the three remaining members of the City Council.

Only one person, Alfred Reid, had applied for the vacancy, but the *Cumberland Evening Times* reported in "whispered conferences held in the nooks in the rotunda" other names were mentioned to become the new police and fire commissioner.

In the council meeting, Commissioner of Finance and Revenue John Stump put forth Reid's name for election as the police and fire commissioner. After a discussion, the vote was taken and it resulted in a 2-2 tie.

Koon then nominated James Walter Thomas, but the vote for him also resulted in a 2-2 tie.

Finally, Commissioner of Water and Electric Lights Charles Cumiskey nominated Anna McCleave, the widow of attorney John McCleave. The nomination surprised those in attendance because a woman had never served on the Cumberland City Council since the council had been seated in 1835.

McCleave was active in civic affairs and had served the Red Cross during World War I. More importantly, she was not without experience, having been appointed by Police Chief Oscar Eyerman as a policewoman to serve in Cumberland, and her authority has never been revoked," the *Cumberland Evening Times* reported.

When the vote was taken McCleave had been elected the new police and fire commissioner 3-1.

Reporters and well-wishers rushed from the council chambers to McCleave's home to get her reaction to the election. She told them she was surprised and found it a "great compliment" but she would wait for official word before she made further comment.

As McCleave pondered whether to accept the appointment, the public began to weigh in on the decision. "Not in years has an appointment to public office attracted as much attention in Cumberland as the naming of Mrs. McCleave," the newspaper reported.

Women were ecstatic at the news. It was a great achievement since women had only received the right to vote two years earlier.

It was also the newness of a woman's right to vote that gave McCleave's opponents fuel to fight her nomination. They said she wasn't a registered city voter so she shouldn't be eligible to serve in office. However, the reason she wasn't registered is because the city hadn't started registering women voters after the U.S. Constitution was amended to allow them the vote.

The newspaper also noted another argument against her, writing, "Certain elements in the city who are deeply interested in the Police Department were loud in the opposition to a woman police commissioner. It was explained that this opposition is based on the assumption that a woman would be hard to 'approach' on matters of policy to prevent a strict observance of certain city ordinances."

McCleave made her decision the following day. "While Mrs. McCleave stated the honor conferred upon her was appreciated, she was unable to accept because of her household duties and other activities, which would make it impossible for her to serve and devote full time to the office," the *Cumberland Evening Times* reported.

So the council members met May 31 and called for nominations to fill the open position. Reid, the only man who had applied for the position, was nominated and this time elected in a 3-1 vote.

With this missed opportunity, a woman would not serve on the Cumberland City Council for another generation, when Lucile Roeder was elected as commissioner of streets and public property in 1950.

This article appeared on the Cumberland Times-News on June 4, 2007.

A hand of "Blackjack"

In 1921, a man many people considered to be the greatest general of the 20th Century took time to honor a man considered the country's greatest general of the 18th Century. And he did it in Cumberland.

General John "Black Jack" Pershing served in the Spanish-American War, the Philippines insurrection, the Mexican Expedition and was the overall American Commander in Europe during World War I. After the war, he served as the Army Chief of Staff.

The Arlington Cemetery web site, *www.arlingtoncemetery.net*, notes in Pershing's biography, "General Pershing is the First World War, and the proof of this lies in the fact that after over fifty years no other general's name comes readily to mind when that war is mentioned."

This almost-single association with World War I is because "Pershing had accomplished the near impossible, whipping an ill-prepared American military into an effective, disciplined, 2 million-member fighting machine in World War I and then leading it to victory as its field commander," Paul Allen wrote in a 2006 article in the *Tucson Citizen*.

By 1921, the City of Cumberland was ready to dedicate George Washington's log cabin headquarters as a historical site at Riverside Park. Washington had used the cabin while he served in the area from 1755 to 1758 and then again in 1794.

Following Washington's use, it had served as a residence until 1844. It had also been at various locations including in front of the county courthouse and on Bedford Road.

However, William J. Morley, the man who restored Washington's headquarters at Valley Forge, Pa., had been hired to restore Cumberland's Washington's headquarters.

WWI General "Blackjack" Pershing rides in a Cumberland parade on April 21, 1921. Courtesy of the Cumberland City Council from the Herman and Stacia Miller Collection.

The *Cumberland Evening Times* noted at the time of the dedication that "...nothing new has been added, except the best tile roof obtainable has been placed upon it to ensure preservation o its priceless parts..." When decayed logs needed to be replaced in the cabin, they weren't replaced with new wood, but with logs taken from the second-oldest house in Cumberland at the time.

With the cabin restored and at its new home, plans were made for a grand celebration.

On April 21, 1921, Pershing, accompanied by his aide Major General G.C. Marshall, Jr. came from Washington, D.C. to Cumberland. They ate lunch at the Ft. Cumberland Hotel for Lunch, then visited city hall to meet with Mayor Thomas Koon and the city council.

At 2 p.m. the parade began to form up and began marching at 3 p.m. The newspaper reported that thousands of people had come into town by car and train to watch the parade.

"The blaring bands, rippling colors, and marching men in eight files deep, presented a thrilling spectacle that aroused patriotic fervor," reported the *Cumberland Evening Times*.

The parade's first division included the municipal band, the color guard, visiting posts of the American Legion and ex-servicemen, McElwees Band of Keyser, the Cumberland American Legion, local wounded veterans and Grand Army of the Republic veterans in cars. The second division included the B&O Railroad shop band, the Cumberland Lodge of Patriots of Order of the Sons of America, the Loyal Order of the Moose and the boys' band.

Pershing rode in a car along with Koon. "Escorted by a guard of honor, composed of ex-service men, who served in combat divisions overseas, armed and wearing the grim trench helmet, the commander of the armies and the marching men representing every branch of the military service were accorded a stirring ovation. Large crowds lined the flag-bedecked streets over which the parade passed from Park Street to Riverside Park," the newspaper reported.

Pershing stopped at Washington Street along with Chief Marshal Arthur Dixon and his assistants George Henderson, John Littlefield, Russell Paupe and William Huster to review the veterans as they marched by him.

He arrived at the crowd massing at Washington Headquarters and delivered a dedication speech honoring a fellow general who was also credited with winning the war he fought in.

Afterwards, Pershing went to Rose Hill and visited with James Walter Thomas and his wife. Later that evening, he attended a banquet in his honor at the Masonic Temple. Maryland Governor Albert Ritchie also came into town to attend the banquet for Pershing.

The following day, the *Cumberland Evening Times* reported, "According to his own testimony, it was a most delightful day for General Pershing, who declared last night that he had been in many cities since returning from France, but in not place had he felt more at home than in Cumberland, Md."

This article appeared in the June/July 2008 issue of Allegany Magazine.

The Georges Creek mining wars

"Scab!"

The accusation rang out against the lone coal miner as he passed near Frostburg's Gunter Hotel one evening in 1923.

The miner didn't mind the words. He had heard worse because of his decision to continue working while so many of his fellow miners were striking.

While the shouts didn't disturb him, the approaching mob of striking miners did. And the gunfire aimed in his direction frightened him.

He ran down Main Street and turned onto Maple Street. He jumped on a motorcycle he had hidden in a barn earlier in the day and escaped the mob.

The *Frostburg Sesquicentennial Souvenir Book* noted this was the last mob violence directed at someone from the Allegany County coal mines.

The 1922-1923 coal miners' strike was a hard-fought effort by the United Mine Workers to unionize county mining operations. In the end, the effort failed and may have brought an early end to coal mining as a major county industry.

"Even though organized labor did not cause the ruin of the Georges Creek coal region, it is nevertheless undeniable that the miner's strike of 1922-23 hastened the end," wrote Harry Stegmaier, Jr. in *Allegany County-A History*.

Previous attempts had been made in 1879, 1882, 1886, 1894 and

1900 to unionize the mines.

A postcard showing the mine entrance to the Appleton Mine in Lonaconing, one of the many coal mines in the Georges Creek Region of Allegany County. Courtesy of the Albert and Angela Feldstein Collection.

"Unions, however, had failed to establish a secure base in the county. Although a large number of miners and a smaller number of laborers and mechanics were sympathetic to unionization, company policy still held sway. Determined to retain their authority, moreover, mining companies would mount a more vigorous counteroffensive against union in the last decade of the nineteenth century," wrote Stegmaier.

Miners even distrusted other miners. During the 1882 strike, the National Knights of Labor failed to financially support striking miners, which weakened the miners' ability to continue striking. County miners remembered this when the 1894 strike call came and some miners refused to strike because they feared the union wouldn't financially back them.

During this strike, Stegmaier wrote, "The division among Allegany miners became a bitter one, involving 'the gentle sex' in not-so-gentle modes of action. Eckhart women accompanied their husband to the mines and threatened to replace men forced out of the mines by strikers. On the other hand, Carlos sisters stoned workers coming out of the tunnels. Frostburg miners encountered sixty women 'armed with tin pans, buckets, baseball bats and babies' as they returned home to work."

Coal was the lifeblood of Georges Creek for decades and the region produced some of the best coal in the world. Maryland coal production peaked in 1907 with 5.5 millions.

"In 1920, just before the onset of postwar depression, the Georges Creek mines produced roughly 4 million tons and employed about 5,500. This was the last of the good years for the region," wrote Kathryn Harvey in *The Best-Dressed Miners*.

A postcard showing the mine entrance to the Koontz Mine near Lonaconing, one of the many coal mines in the Georges Creek Region of Allegany County. Courtesy of the Albert and Angela Feldstein Collection.

On April 1, 1922, the UMW called a national strike. Many mines had low pay and poor working conditions, though according to Harvey, the Allegany County miners "were said to be generally satisfied with their wages and working conditions." However, Harvey notes different companies were found to be underpaying their miners for the amount of coal they mined by using light scales.

Though the county miners were non-union, they walked out in support. When the national strike ended August 15, the Allegany County miners stayed out in an effort to win union recognition. The UMW supported the strikers with $750,000 and a food commissary in Frostburg. The mining companies, for their part, brought in strikebreakers from Cleveland, Pittsburgh and West Virginia. Guards were armed with automatic weapons and even submachine guns, according to Stegmaier.

A photo showing the mine entrance to the Ocean Mine in Midland, one of the many coal mines in the Georges Creek Region of Allegany County. Courtesy of the Albert and Angela Feldstein Collection.

He wrote, "This explosive situation was further complicated when many of the local miners who did not agree with continuing the strike went back to work. Strikers threatened reprisals against them and their families. Violence was bound to occur, and it soon did."

In August 1923, Harry Martin, a Consolidation Coal Company

mine guard, was charged with throwing a grenade into a crowd of picketers.

Later that month, George Porter of Zihlman was shot and killed while driving his motorcycle to work at a Mount Savage and George's Creek Coal Company mine. W.H. Walbert of Consolidation Coal Company was eventually charged with the murder.

Walbert was also shot in the incident. He was taken to Miner's Hospital for treatment, but according to the *Cumberland Evening Times*, "it was decided later to remove him to Cumberland as there is said to have aroused much feeling over the shooting of Porter and [Walbert] might run afoul a mob." He went to Western Maryland Hospital where he stayed under guard.

In another incident, Frank Miller of Gilmore was shot and wounded while driving to work at a mine. Martin was also charged in this shooting. Unknown assailants later fired shots into his house. "At this particular point, it is declared by eyewitnesses, there was a volley [of shots]," reported the *Cumberland Evening Times*.

Stegmaier wrote, "Violence became so prevalent that the Allegany County grand jury, after considering the numerous cases of assault and intimidation, recommended that a special constabulary be formed to preserve order. The grand jury described conditions, particularly in Frostburg and Midland, as 'a disgrace to the county.'"

The UMW called off the nearly 20-month strike in November 1923 without unionizing the mines.

What did happen was many miners lost their jobs not only because the mining companies were careful about rehiring, but because the strike helped cripple the mining industry in the area. Between 1923 and 1930, 27 mining companies went out of business in the Georges Creek Region. Even the union suffered, losing more than 60 percent of its membership in the region by the end of the strike.

A shorter version of this article appeared in the December 2006/ January2007 issue of Allegany Magazine.

How the flood of 1924 all but dried up the C&O Canal

When Pat Boyer docked his Canal Towage Company boat No. 5 in the Cumberland Basin of the Chesapeake and Ohio Canal near the end of November 1923, he didn't know he was marking the end of an era had ended. He had dropped off a load of coal in Georgetown and made it back to Cumberland before the canal was drained for the winter. With No. 5 already in the basin, he would be one of the first boats loaded when once next spring came and the boating season started.

Next spring came, but the boating season didn't.

What did come was rain. On March 28 and 29, 1924, heavy rains pelted the area helping to melt the snow on the mountains. All that melted snow and rain ran into the creeks and Potomac River.

"By 8:30 a.m. on the 29th, Wills Creek overflowed its banks resulting in tremendous havoc and property loss in the Cumberland vicinity. Telephone, telegraph and electric wires were swept away and the city left in darkness. Cumberland's central business district was flooded to a height of four feet. Most of the paving washed away with a torrent of water rushing down Mechanic Street at a great velocity," wrote local historian Al Feldstein in the historical commentary of my novel *The Rain Man.*

Contemporary newspaper reports said the waters were rising as fast as 30 inches an hour and approaching the then-record crest of the 1889 flood that had helped put the canal's rival the Baltimore and Ohio Railroad in control of it when the canal went into receivership.

A lock of the C&O Canal is nearly empty of water in 1938. Courtesy of U.S. Department of the Interior.

When the 1924 floodwaters receded, the damage was assessed. "There was really little destruction outside of the canal, which had been badly mauled at Cumberland where the torrent in the river had leveled some of the banks. The dams survived the onslaught of the river fairly well, and the lower valley escaped serious damage altogether," wrote Walter Sanderlin in *The Great National Project*.

While the canal could have been repaired as it had been after previous floods, the B&O Railroad Company chose not to do so. The canal was a burden to railroad company. It needed the use of the canal rights of way, but the courts had ordered that the railroad needed to operate the canal profitably or lose its charter. With only about $50,000 a year being collected in tolls, Mike High wrote in The C&O Canal Companion that the B&O "most assuredly not fulfilling the court's stipulation that it continue to show a profit to hold its charter."

In a 1979 interview featured in Home on the Canal, Lester Mose, Sr. who had worked on the canal during its last years, said, "It could be that something else interfered with them; but in '22 the canal didn't do much, and in '23 they done very little. I worked at Pinesburg and I was out there right along the canal and I could walk out there and look at it. Once in a while you'd see a boat go by, but not too many."

Another canaller, George Hooper Wolfe, wrote in *I Drove Mules on*

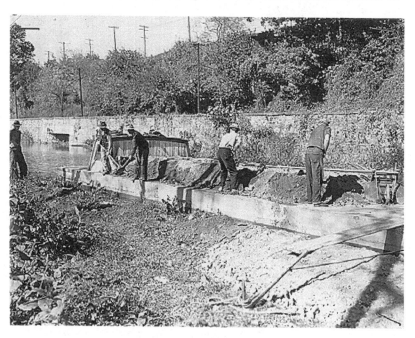

A maintenance crew repairs a washout along the C&O Canal. Courtesy of the U.S. Department of the Interior.

the C&O Canal, "The railroad saw in this an opportunity to relieve itself of the expense of further operation. Enough repairs were made to assert that the Canal was a going concern, with enough revenues from the Georgetown factories and dams along the river to pay the expenses of a minimum operating staff; and it was also maintained that the Canal could be placed in operation quickly if business warranted. The court went along with this fiction, and the B&O retained the property, but without having any further expenses for its maintenance."

Some boats hauled sand from Georgetown to the power plant that was being constructed in Williamsport for a few months in 1924, but the damage at the Cumberland end kept boats away. Boyer's No. 5 had been the last boat to haul freight on the canal.

Mose said, "The '24 flood took all the boats away. What wasn't taken away in '24 [the] '36 [flood] cleaned them up. There wasn't nothing there. It was dead. Closed up and growed up with trees."

The canal had originally reached Cumberland in 1850 and it ended there unintentionally because of competition from the B&O and ended there forever 74 years later because of an intentional decision by the B&O.

The B&O sold its rights to the canal to the federal government in August 1938 for $2 million. It was a paper transaction that allowed the railroad to pay off some of its $80 million loan from the governments Reconstruction Finance Corp and to borrow another $8.2 million more.

Otho Swain was born on the canal in 1901 and worked on it during its final years. He said in a 1976 interview, "The canal finally closed down in 1924. There was flood damage then, but the railroad—it was the railroad that really killed the canal."

This article appeared in the April 2007 issue of Allegany Magazine.

Half-century-old Main Street store destroyed by fire

A little after 5 a.m. on March 12, 1925, Frostburg Police Officer Thomas Griffith smelled smoke.

He hurried down East Main Street trying to follow the scent of burning wood. He hadn't gone far when he saw the flames piercing the windows of Hitchins Brothers Department Store.

The store had been in business for more than half a century and employed 45 people. The first floor carried groceries, shoes and general merchandise. The second floor had clothing for men, women and children, home furnishings and floor coverings. The third floor was the stock and supply room.

Griffith sent in the fire call, but when the Frostburg firefighters arrived, it was clear they would need help. Calls for assistance went out to Cumberland, Lonaconing and Midland.

As the Frostburg firefighters began battling the blaze, Griffith woke Upton Edwards, the assistant manager at the department store. Together, they entered the store around 5:30 a.m. hoping to find the source of the fire. They got as far as the stairway to the third floor when the heat, smoke and fire drove them back.

The firefighters were having their own problems. Fire Chief Bernard Hughes and John Pritchard advanced across the first floor wetting everything down. The heavy pressure from a new four-million gallon reservoir kicked in, knocking both men to the floor as the water surged through the hose.

Despite being able to put water further into the building with the increased pressure, the fire spread to the entire building. The *Cumberland Evening Times* reported, "The flames burst from the roof, throwing burning sparks and embers high in the air."

Luckily, there was no wind, which helped in the firefighters' efforts to save the adjoining buildings and contain the flames.

Fire Chief Reid Hoenicka made the run up the mountain in 20 minutes in Cumberland's fire engine No. 1 and arrived shortly before six o'clock. The engines from Lonaconing and Midland arrived shortly after Cumberland.

This is Main Street in Frostburg as it appeared early in the 20th Century. Hitchins Brothers Department Store is the three-story building on the left. Courtesy of the Albert and Angela Feldstein Collection.

The firefighters had to work around the growing crowd that sometimes blocked their paths to the building despite the intense heat coming from the fire.

The newspaper reported, "Taking position on the side, front and rear, the firemen deluged the burning building from every point of vantage."

By 7 a.m., the fire was under control. Despite the walls of the building collapsing, the Hafer building on the north side, the Palace Theatre on the south side and St. Michael Church across the street were all saved from damage.

Emory Hitchins, the manager of the store, went around and personally thanked all the firefighters for their efforts in trying to save his store.

The building and its contents were listed as a total loss with the building valued at at least $150,000 and the stock and equipment valued at $200,000.

Faulty wiring was thought to have started the blaze sometime after midnight on March 11 because a final store inspection had been made at 11 p.m. on March 11 by Shoe Department Manager Joseph Condon as he closed up the store for the night.

In a stroke of good luck, the store's steel safe was found in the basement. It was stored on the third floor but when the fire weakened the floors enough, it fell through to the basement. The safe was opened and all of the money and documents inside were found intact.

The business resumed in the Hitchens-Watts-Hitchens building and part of the Citizen's Bank Building, pending Hitchins building a bigger and better department store.

This article appeared in the Cumberland Times-News on May 17, 2004.

The "Babe" comes to Cumberland

Baseball in Cumberland was struggling in 1931, leading some to speculate if it would even survive. Cumberland's once-popular minor-league team, the Colts, just couldn't draw the fans to the stadium any longer. On September 1, the *Cumberland Evening Times* reported that for the Colts game with Beaver Falls "Only 51 paid their way in and the players practically had the lot to themselves."

Two days later, a miracle came to town. His name was George Herman Ruth but people just called him Babe.

"He is the strongest hitter in baseball and that shouldn't be the case. Statistically, it should be impossible that an early 20th Century athlete should continue to dominate over late 20th century athletes," said Bill Jenkinson, author of *The Year Babe Hit 104 Home Runs*.

Because the Colts were a farm team of the Yankees, the team owners arranged an exhibition game to breathe new life into Cumberland's minor league team.

"His powerful home-run bat has lured thousands and thousands of people into the stadiums of the major league and his worth cannot be measured by his annual yearly salary of $85,000," reported the *Cumberland Evening Times*.

The New York Yankees arrived in Cumberland at 8:30 a.m. on a Thursday morning. They greeted the crowd at the Western Maryland Railway Station as they hopped off the train and headed down the stairs to waiting cabs. They went right to breakfast at the Algonquin

Hotel and then to their rooms to rest before that afternoon's exhibition game with the Cumberland Colts, a Yankee's farm team.

Babe Ruth following through after swinging a bat, standing on the field at Comiskey Park. Courtesy of the Library of Congress.

Despite a strict command to hotel management that none of the players be disturbed until 1 p.m., fans still lingered in the lobby all morning in the hopes of catching sight of Ruth or his teammates. The Cumberland Evening Times reported, "Babe Ruth and Lou Gehrig, the home run twins, are supposed to have gone for a stroll after eating breakfast but traffic was not tied up anywhere along the main stems and on those premises, it is reasonable to believe that the Babe and his playmate also stayed within the confines of the hotel."

The Yankees also passed up opportunities to tour the Celanese and Kelly-Springfield plants and receive gifts from the workers. Their game was at 3 p.m. and they needed to rest. Mark Roth, the Yankees' road secretary, had eight trunks of playing equipment taken to the Community Stadium near Wineow Street. Most of the weight in the trunks was made up of 100 bats the Yankees used.

About the time the Yankees were being roused from their rooms, the gates to Community Park opened and the crowd quickly filled the bleachers. "With Community Stadium creaking under the weight of nearly 3,900 fans and with adjoining sheds, railroad trestles and house roofs taken up by thousands of others, the New York Yankees illustrated why they are called baseball's biggest showmen," the newspaper noted.

The Colts came onto the field and practiced batting while the Yankees tossed the baseball around in front of their dugout. Then the Yankees got their turn at the plate. Ruth was the third batter up and the crowd cheered, although it was only pregame batting practice. Former Cumberland Times-News Sports Editor Suter Kegg wrote, "Ruth belted a ball over the distant centerfield fence, the only player ever to accomplish the feat."

The lucky youth who fought with his friends to get the ball was John "Boots" Sapp. Sapp also had Babe and Lou Gehrig autograph the ball. Sapp's daughter Shirley Shaffer still owns the ball. She keeps it in a safe-deposit box.

The exhibition game began a few minutes before its scheduled start time at three o'clock. Gordon Rhodes pitched for the Yankees and Vito Tamulis pitched for the Colts. The Yankees scout had made certain that the Colts had a "safe" pitcher "so the big timers would not be in too much danger or be forced to do too much dodging."

The Yankees came to bat first. Earle Combs hit a single into centerfield. Myril Hoag hit a fly ball to become the first out of the game.

Then the legend came to the plate. Taking a "meek" swing (a half-cut) at Tamulis' pitch, Ruth sent the ball over the right field wall. Watching the ball go over the fence, Ruth turned to the Yankees' bench and told his teammates, "They ought to have thrown in a piece of iron."

"The Babe gave them all they wanted, in fact, the one thing the majority cared about most. He poled a homer over the right field wall on the first ball pitched to him in his first time at bat," the newspaper noted. And, "Late in the game, he nearly turned Buddy Hall inside out with a fiery smash to center."

Ruth showed Cumberland a glimpse at why he was considered the greatest player the game has known. The Yankees went on to win the game 5-1. They left Cumberland at 8:40 p.m. on a train out of the Queen City Station and they left behind some of the magic and legend of Babe Ruth that is still remembered today.

"What a difference a few stars make, it took the biggest club in baseball's brightlights to bring out the fact that Cumberland is far from a has-been habitat of the national pastime but the 3836 people who paid admission to yesterday's exhibition game between the Yanks and Colts surely stamped the Queen City as a baseball burg," the paper noted the next day.

A shorter version of this article appeared in the Cumberland Times-News on July 12, 2004.

A 10-pound boy
named "Oxygen"

Mrs. Hutson screamed with the final effort to push her son into the world on June 12, 1932. Exhausted, she collapsed back onto her bed that was now damp with the sweat from her labor. The doctor announced that the baby was a boy. He cut the umbilical cord and swatted the baby on the bottom to start him crying.

The cries started, but they were weak, not the full-throated wail a 10-pound baby should have been able to make.

Though undiagnosed at the time, the baby may have had transient tachypnea. While in the womb, babies get their oxygen from the blood vessels of the placenta. Their lungs are full of fluid. They begin to clear the fluid in response to hormonal changes shortly before they are born. More fluid is squeezed out of their lungs during the birthing process, and the remainder gets coughed out after birth. A baby with transient tachypnea clears his lungs too slowly, causing breathing difficulties. The baby breathes harder and faster trying to get enough oxygen.

This is what was happening with the newborn baby.

When Mrs. Hutson asked to hold her newborn son, the doctor said that she would have to wait.

Kitzmiller, where the Hutsons lived, was one of the larger coal-mining towns along the Upper Potomac in 1932. In its heyday, Kitzmiller had a bank, bakery, theater, hotel, post office and stores, but it never had a hospital.

However, a hospital is what the baby needed. While in most instances a home birth wouldn't be a problem, it was now. The baby was struggling to breathe and without the right equipment, the type of equipment found at a hospital, the little guy might not survive.

L.C. Hutson, far right, used his experience with mine rescue equipment to help save the life of his newborn son in 1932. Courtesy of *www.whilbr.com*.

The closest hospital was Miner's Hospital in Frostburg, but the doctor worried the baby might not survive the journey.

L.C. Hutson, the baby's father, was a vocational mining instructor and he had another idea. The baby needed oxygen and Hutson knew how to get it. He and the doctor placed a call to Mine Inspector Powers and Assistant Vocational Mining Instructor Ewing in Frostburg. They brought an inhalator from the Frostburg Mine Rescue Station to Kitzmiller.

"A surgeon and nurse were present and Messrs. Powers and Ewing, assisted by Mr. Hutson, gave oxygen to the babe and revived him," reported the *Cumberland Sunday Times*. "The babe, a fine 10-pound boy, has been nicknamed 'Oxygen,' a memorial to the occasion."

Garrett County would eventually get a hospital, but not until Oxygen was an adult in 1950. That is when George W. Loar bequeathed

$175,000 to Garrett County to build a hospital. The Garrett County Memorial Hospital was a 30-bed facility with an emergency room, laboratory, X-ray department and operating room when it first opened.

Five years later, 20 more beds were added to accommodate the growing need for hospital services in the region.

Story update: Charles "Oxygen" Hutson is now a 76-year-old great-grandfather who has been married for 52 years. He splits his time between west Texas and Garrett County.

This article appeared in the Cumberland Times-News on April 5, 2009.

It wasn't a spaceship that landed at Mexico Farms

Look! Up in the sky! It's a bird! It's a plane! It's ... an autogyro?

On Thursday afternoon, Oct. 22, 1931, the people on the streets of Cumberland stopped what they were doing and looked skyward. They pointed at the strange object in the sky and murmured to each other. Some people panicked, wondering if they were seeing some sort of spaceship. What they were seeing was the autogyro attracting attention for the air show at the Mexico Farms Airfield.

The *Cumberland Evening Times* reported, "A forerunner of the show was the appearance over the city yesterday of the autogyro, the latest type of flying ship, which rises and lands vertically, and can be made stationary when aloft."

Unlike a helicopter, the autogyro used an unpowered rotor that turned as the autogyro was pulled through the air by a separate powered propeller. The vehicle was the invention of Spanish engineer Juan de la Cierva in 1923.

This particular model had arrived from New York on Thursday and was promptly flown around the city by pilot Jack Bear of Middletown, N.Y. The autogyro cost $20,000 or the equivalent of $250,000 today. Because of the expense and the lack of a hangar at Mexico Farms, the autogyro was flown to Hagerstown each evening and stored there during the three days of the air show.

In addition to autogyro demonstrations, the air show featured wing walkers, parachutists, air acrobatics, spot landing competitions and an

An autogyro like the one that flew over Cumberland in 1931 impresses a crowd at an air derby at the Washington Dover Airport. Courtesy of the Hiller Aircraft Museum.

air parade.

The low point of the event was that high winds on Sunday caused the air events to be postponed. During the lull in excitement, several aviators got an idea for how to spice things up.

"Several aviators on the field were entertaining the crowd with a captive parachute, flying it like a kite. The parachute was attached to an automobile in the field. It would soar into the air and several aviators caught the rope and rose into the air with it," reported the *Cumberland Evening Times*.

Unfortunately, 16-year-old Frances Portmess of Cumberland decided to get into the fun. He grabbed onto the dangling rope like the other aviators, but Portmess' rope snapped while he was 30 feet off the ground. Portmess hit the ground, fracturing his ribs and a couple vertebrae. He also got a concussion. Not being Superman, he was rushed to Memorial Hospital in critical condition.

This article appeared in the Cumberland Times-News on August 2, 2004.

Slots machines have been legal in Maryland on two occasions

As Marylanders prepare to vote on whether slot machines should be allowed in the state, there have been two other times when they were legal in the state. Once was in the late 1800's to the 1930's and the other time was the 1940's to the 1960's.

When slot machines were banned in Maryland from 1937 to 1939, it fell upon local law enforcement officials to enforce the ban, although many local politicians frequented the clubs that had slot machines.

"One of the first official acts State's Attorney Morgan C. Harris, according to local officers, was a warning to social and fraternal clubs that all slot machines must be removed," reported the *Cumberland Sunday Times* on June 13, 1937.

Many mechanical gaming devices were invented in American in the 1890's in NY, including the first nickel in the slot device. Charles Fey and Gustav Schultze and Theodore Holtz are the one who are credited with making the first true slot machine. Then in 1899 Fey developed the Liberty Bell slot machine that used 3 reels with various symbols and the distinctive handle on the side and coin tray on bottom.

California was the first state to try and ban slot machines in 1909, not because of a moral issue but because lawmakers couldn't regulate them so that the state made money.

With the onset of World War I, the slot machine industry nearly died. Business had been dropping off with various states banning slot machines so the machines were being sold for scrap metal. Then the slot machine manufacturers began shutting down their production to switch over to producing weapons for the U.S. military.

The Liberty Bell slot machine was the first slot machine that was recognizeable as the same type of machine still used today. Courtesy of Wikimedia Commons.

Following the war, slot machines and illegal booze both found fertile ground in the 1920's speakeasies. This allowed politicians to begin criminalizing slot machines because they were owned by criminals. The Great Depression allowed politicians to paint slots as robbing from people who could ill afford it. In addition, since slot machines were in speakeasies, the illegal bars where liquor was sold despite prohibition, lawmakers could easily make the case that gambling was a mobster-run activity.

Harris issued his ultimatum to one club to use as an example since it was common knowledge that the private clubs had slots for their members, including many local politicians.

"The presence of the nickel, dime and quarter contraptions was 'embarrassing' to the public officials, who in recent months have taken steps to prohibit them. Some lodge and club members contend the machines were on private 'property, and 'there is nothing morally wrong' in them; because only members can play them, and no minors are permitted to operate "the machines," reported the *Cumberland Sunday*

Times.

One club admitted to making $3000 profit on slot machines in 1936 (about $45,000). Interestingly, the newspaper noted that one of the principal objections to the machines was that "many women became addicted to playing them." No mention was made that men could be addicted to them, too.

The *Cumberland Sunday Times* reported that news traveled fast. Although only one club had been told to remove its slot machines, most of the clubs that the newspaper visited had them removed within a couple days. The clubs had gotten the message in Harris's first warning to the clubs.

Though Maryland had lifted its ban by the beginning of World War II, that was not the case for most states. When a 1950 law banned the shipment of slot machines to states where they were illegal, only Nevada, Idaho and Maryland were able to receive slot machines.

This article appeared in the Cumberland Times-News on October 1, 2008.

All they knew was that it filled their empty bellies

Elementary school students at Hammond Street Elementary in Westernport filed through the lunch line receiving plates of hot roast beef, mashed potatoes and green beans. They didn't realize they were also receiving service from a premier food service operation. They only knew it was a warm lunch that filled their sometimes-empty bellies.

"Qualified school authorities and nutrition experts have stated in recent months that the lunch system adopted in Allegany County schools is second to none in the country and in fact is far superior to similar systems in schools throughout Ohio, Pennsylvania, West Virginia and a number of other states," The *Cumberland News* reported in September 1945.

The reason for the praise is that most schools at the time had no cafeteria operation. Children instead brought their lunches to school in a lunch box. When there was cafeteria staff to serve lunches, it was generally a cafeteria director who cooked and prepared the food, assisted by older students who served lunches to students in large city schools.

Allegany County changed that concept not only for the county but for the country.

In August 1944, the board of education requested a part-time nutritionist from the Cumberland and Allegheny Gas Co. Nutritionist Flora Dowler was sent to assist the board and W.P. Cooper, the food program director for the board, who was already a pioneer in school food service.

Dowler's work began with two days of training for the cooks at Fort Hill High School where she demonstrated and prepared different types of lunches that met state guidelines and could be prepared on premise. She followed that up with similar visits to each school at least once a month.

Students at East Side Elementary line up for school lunches in the 1940s. Serving lunch in elementary school was a unique concept pioneered by the Allegany County Food Service Association beginning in 1939. The glass milk bottles on the tables were recycled for repeated use. Cardboard milk cartons were introduced in the 1950s. Courtesy of the Allegany County Food Service Association.

During those visits, she discovered a lunch program that had been started in 1939 in Hammond Street Elementary School. The board, working with the Works Progress Administration, the Surplus Marketing Corp., Maryland Department of Public Welfare and the school's Parent Teacher Association provided free lunches to 60 percent of the students at the school.

Dowler said this was needed because "most of the bus children attending this school came from the region where the coal mines were practically abandoned and the parents unemployed."

The program's success led to its expansion to all other schools in the county.

"This beginning has resulted in offering hot lunches daily to three-quarters of the school children in the county," said Dowler.

The program was able to operate on a county-wide basis because of support from the War Food Administration and the Maryland Department of Public Health. The War Food Administration provided financial support and food. The Department of Public Health examined the 76 cafeteria employees and inspected the lunch rooms to make sure they were sanitary.

At the time, cafeterias weren't available in every school. Four schools served their students lunch in the auditorium, and students at Corriganville Elementary ate lunch in their classrooms.

Columbia Street School was the only school where there wasn't a lunch program and that was because there was no space for a cafeteria. However, by 1945, work was under way to remedy this problem.

Once the program was expanded county wide, 26 schools served 8,400 type A lunches daily, 14 schools served 3,300 type C milk lunches daily and 20 percent of the county's 15,000 students were receiving free or reduced-price lunches.

The cost of a school lunch was 60 cents a week or 15 cents daily. More than 2 million lunches were served in Allegany County schools during the 1944-1945 school year.

"Although no scientific research has been conducted to prove the value of this program, teachers, county nurses and principals feel the need for it and are most gratified with the results of the program to date. Some tests have been made in various schools and results indicate better health, better school attendance and improved scholarship," said Dowler.

For her work in pioneering the new cafeteria system, Dowler received the annual McCall Magazine award for outstanding work in her field.

This article appeared in the Cumberland Times-News on August 30, 2004.

The French sculptor from Lonaconing

To George Conlon, the egg was the pinnacle of evolution ... at least in terms of the shape of the human head.

"Don't laugh at the hen," Conlon said in a 1927 interview. "She has evolved from the egg; the American is evolving Into one. Take a large egg in one hand and a mirror in the other. If you cannot readily distinguish between the two reflections, then you're 100 percent American; the ovoid ancestor of the 110 percent Americans with which the United States will, within the next few hundred years, be filled."

Conlon believed that because of the mix of cultures in America, American heads were becoming egg shaped. He would be someone who would have known, too. In his day, Conlon, a native of Lonaconing, achieved fame in America and Europe for his sculptures of famous figures.

Among his subjects were Clarence Darrow, Charles Lindbergh, Blackjack Pershing, Amelia Earhart and Will Rogers.

"A sculptor, you know, learns to read a man's character and possibilities from the shape of the skull," Conlon once said.

Conlon was born in Lonaconing to working-class family. As a young man, he worked in the Georges Creek coal mines. It is there he is began to discover his artistic talents.

"There the aspiring artist was reported to have made a bust of Maryland Governor Edwin Warfield from the plastic clay that was used to plug holes in the mine walls. Impressed by the portrait, the governor helped Conlon launch his art career," according to the U.S. Senate web site.

Conlon attended the Maryland Institute College of Art in Baltimore and won the Rinehart Scholarship that allowed him to study at the Academie Julian and the Academie Colarossi in Paris.

This bust of Cordell Hull, former U.S. Secretary of State and "Father of the U.N.," is on permanent display in the U.S. Capitol. It was sculpted by Lonaconing native George Conlon and presented to Congress as a gift from the *Cumberland Evening Times* and Conlon in December 1944.

He married Mary Wilhowska in 1926 and they lived together in his Paris studio. The Nazis began their occupation of France in May 1940 and the Conlons obtained passports to return to America in June 1941. When George got the passports, he wife was visiting her sick mother in southern France. She remained with her mother planning to take a later ship to America. He lost contact with her after December 7, 1941 when the U.S. and France broke off communications. Mary Conlon died in June 1943 without ever seeing her husband again.

At the end of the war, Conlon sculpted a bust of Cordell Hull, former U.S. Secretary of State and "Father of the U.N." Conlon said he thought the shape of Hull's head made him an excellent subject for a sculpture.

Senator Tydings of Maryland presented the bronze bust to Congress as a gift from the *Cumberland Evening Times* and Conlon. The bust is still on permanent display in the Capitol Building.

"In a joint resolution, adopted on December 4, 1944, Congress authorized the Joint Committee on the Library to accept the newspaper's gift. The bronze bust of Cordell Hull was unveiled in the Senate Reception Room the following year," according to the U.S. Senate web site.

Conlon died in his sleep in his Washington D.C. home on December 14, 1980 at the age of 92.

This article appeared in the Cumberland Times-News on December 15, 2008.

No overalls in sight: Cumberland life surprises city girl from Boston

Cumberland is about 550 miles from Boston by car but it might as well have been another world as far as Evelyn Weissman was concerned in November 1941. She was 24 years old and had spent most of her life in Boston, but big life changes had put her on the train to Cumberland. She remembered joking with her college-graduate friends when she told them that she was visiting Cumberland. "I wonder if I should wear overalls," she had said.

Now she was close to finding out the answer.

The first life change was her boyfriend of two years, Harry Kauffman. She had admired his intelligence and had fallen in love with his kind nature and friendly smile. Now she would soon become Evelyn Kauffman.

Harry was the reason that Evelyn was making this trip. His family had lived in Cumberland since 1927. Now it was time for her to meet the people to whom she would soon be related. With Harry going into the service, they had decided to get married sooner rather than later.

"We'll be arriving in Cumberland soon," the conductor told her as he walked down the aisle.

Evelyn just nodded. The other major change to her life was that Uncle Sam had sent "greetings" to Harry but had graciously allowed him to complete his degree at Harvard Law School. He would be graduating at the age of 23 and then entering the U.S. Army.

Harry and Evelyn had decided that if, by chance, Harry was granted any leave during his training, it would be easier for him to visit all of his family in Cumberland. So the Boston city girl was about to become the Cumberland country girl.

The train squealed to a stop in front of the Queen City Station. Evelyn stepped onto the platform and saw Harry waving to her. He hurried over to her and hugged her tightly, then kissed her.

"Welcome to your new home," Harry said.

This is Cumberland? Evelyn thought.

A shot of Baltimore Street as seen from Emmanuel Episcopal Church around the time of this article. Courtesy of the Albert and Angela Feldstein Collection.

She looked at the Queen City Station and marveled at the building. Harry had described the four-story station to her. It was built from brick with floral wrought-iron verandas and formal gardens.

Harry took Evelyn's hand and they walked to the parking lot. He had the porter put the luggage in the trunk of his car and tipped him. Then he and Evelyn climbed into the car.

"Let me show you the town before we go see my family," Harry suggested.

"I guess if I'm going to live here, I'd better get to know it," Evelyn replied.

He headed down Baltimore Street and the car slowed down about the same time that Evelyn's mouth dropped open. The street was not only packed with cars but crowds of people thronged the sidewalks. And there were no overalls in sight. These people were all dressed impeccably. The Allegany High School oral history book *Work and Wait: Allegany County: The Home Front Years 1941-1945* describes downtown Cumberland this way: "People would visit downtown, not just to make purchases, but also to promenade up and down the street. Several respondents reported that people would often dress in stylish clothes to appear on Baltimore Street. Window-shopping was reported to be a favorite activity of all age groups.

"While Baltimore Street featured the largest department stores, Centre, Mechanic, and Liberty streets provided many locally owned specialty shops. A typical day on Centre Street would find adult customers shopping at Stacey's Produce Market while the children were next door at the popular Hill's Toy Store. Bill Hill, employee, recalls his store sometimes resembled what today would be called a day care center as kids would spend long periods of time there without parental supervision. Homeowners would talk with Mr. Bernstein at his furniture store while other shoppers visited butcher shops trying to secure meat that was limited by wartime rationing. If one walked from Stacey's Market to 'Little Frederick Street,' he would intersect with North Liberty Street where food and beverages were available at the Liberty Tavern, hot dogs at Coney Island, and a movie at the Liberty."

Evelyn took in all of the stores and their names: Manhattan Men's Clothing, Rosenbaum's Department Store, Peskin's Shoes and Clothing, Martin's Women's Clothing and Lazarus Women's Clothing and Restaurant. It was a shopper's paradise that rivaled anything in Boston.

As Harry and Evelyn neared the west end of the street, Harry'' hand darted to the right, pointing to one of the stores. "That's Cumberland Cloak and Suit. Dad opened it in 1927."

His arm flipped almost immediately to the left. "That's the Embassy Theatre. Dad built it in 1930."

How could Cumberland be doing so well when people in Boston were suffering through a Depression where people survived by being given bread on the street? With the elegance she saw here, perhaps that was why Cumberland had been named the Queen City.

This article appeared in the Cumberland Times-News on June 8, 2004.

Shopping was encouraged because shortages lay ahead

In the time of "peace on earth, goodwill to men," the world was at war and men were dying in December 1941.

As Thanksgiving 1941 approached, the war in Europe was on people's minds but it wasn't the dominant story of the day. The county was more concerned about a coal strike that had started in Pennsylvania and was spreading around the country. At times, it appeared more dangerous to Americans than the war. The headlines on the *Cumberland Evening Times* the day after Thanksgiving showed Allegany County's priorities:

GUNS CONTINUE TO BLAZE IN MINE STRIKE
Roosevelt Indicates Federal Action Is Probable
BRITISH-AXIS SHOWDOWN IN LIBYA NEAR

The day before Thanksgiving, an editorial in the Cumberland Evening Times noted, "Although some American ships have been sunk, some American lives have been lost and we are far nearer war than we have been at any time since the new conflagration was lighted in Europe, we are in a manner of speaking, still at peace. Whether this condition will continue we do not know, but at least we should be thankful for the blessings we enjoy at present."

And so they did.

The Christmas season kicked into gear with ads for sales and specials for stores like Rosenbaum's and Lazarus. However, early shopping was encouraged because shortages were expected before the end of the year. Plans were made for a gala on Dec. 27 to honor servicemen from the area. It was thought that about 1,000 of them would be able to get passes to return to Cumberland for the celebration.

That was before Dec. 7.

After the Japanese attacked Pearl Harbor, the United States became a country formally at war. The focus shifted to war-time production of goods and raising a fighting army. Even the coal strike, which had caused so much worry at Thanksgiving, was set aside as miners were drafted and the union and management agreed to work together for war production.

Though not a heavy presence in daily life at this point, what presence there was was growing and the newspaper noted that it put a "damper" on the holiday celebrations. Notes about the selection of air raid wardens for 26 different areas of the city crept in among the notices about holiday parties. Even editorial cartoons reflected both the holiday and the war. The city's first black-out test was conducted the day after Christmas with every home and business within a 10-mile radius of Cumberland expected to douse their lights for 15 minutes once the warning went out.

While a gift-buying boom is expected at Christmas, Christmas 1941 saw another boom. "'War brides' brought a boom yesterday at the marriage license bureau with Court House clerks swamped with altar-bound couples before noon, and the usual Christmas business for Dan Cupid will be increased by khaki-clad young men getting married while home on brief furloughs," reported the Cumberland Sunday Times. The newspaper noted that 49 couples applied for licenses on Dec. 20.

The city also organized a civil air patrol to protect the skies over Allegany County. About 100 pilots in the area volunteered to help in this endeavor. The need was only heightened when two days before Christmas bombers were seen flying over the city. Fortunately, they were American bombers on maneuvers.

Not so fortunate was the report from the WPA supervisor in the area that a cache of dynamite at the airport was tampered with. "Fifth column" sabotage was suspected and the dynamite was moved.

The newspaper tried to put everything in perspective for its readers with an editorial that read, in part: "It is important that we bring about a condition of worldly peace and that this may be accomplished we must vanquish those responsible for its disruption. The thought of Christmas and all that it means should strengthen us in this task. If we are to make such a peace enduring, then we must cultivate that spirit of good will without which there can be no real peace. If we do not do this, then all our sacrifice, all our anguish, all our suffering shall have been in vain. If during this Christmas season we seek that peace of which the herald angels sang, then we can hope for that lasting peace promised unto us. So it is not incongruous to observe Christmas in time of war for the peace of Christmas is in the heart."

This article appeared in the Cumberland Times-News in December 2007.

When the world war came to Allegany County

During World War II, German soldiers marched through French streets, fought in North African deserts and cut wood in Allegany County forests. Hundreds of German soldiers spent the final years of the War to End All Wars in Green Ridge State Forest.

With the Allied success in North Africa in 1943, more than 130,000 POWs were shipped to the U.S. The total eventually reached about 426,000, according to a 1945 Monthly Labor Review.

Franz Boehm was one of those POWs. A Czechoslovakian, Boehm was drafted into the army when Germany annexed the country in 1940. After being wounded on the Russian Front, Boehm was sent to North Africa. He was captured in 1942 after General Rommel's defeat.

Boehm was interned at various U.S. prison camps, but in June 1944, he was shipped from Camp Meade to Camp Flintstone in Allegany County.

In 1943, the Hancock Apple Growers Association applied to the War Food Administration to use POWs as fruit pickers. Many fruit pickers were soldiers and the workload was too great for the remaining workers. The request was approved and the former Civilian Conservation Corp camp in Green Ridge became Camp Flintstone.

While the old forestry camp was designed to house a large group of men, it wasn't designed to hold prisoners.

"Fifteen Mile Creek Road ran right through the camp and they had to relocate it," said Augustine Diaz, who served as a camp guard.

The road was gated off through the camp and re-routed around the camp.

Camp Flintstone housed around 250 prisoners with 40 U.S. soldiers to watch over them, according to Diaz.

"They had six or seven barracks enclosed in barb wire. They had a dining hall and rec room. We had two towers and two shacks, officers quarters, latrines, a medical building and a supply room," Diaz said.

A view of Camp Flintstone POW Camp through the fencing.

He was one of three Allegany County natives who were part of the Camp Flintstone guard detail. The other two were Bill Byrnes of Frostburg and Bill George of Cumberland. Diaz is the only one still living.

When Diaz arrived at Camp Flintstone in 1944, Boehm was already a prisoner there.

"The prisoners were used in the orchards in and around Hancock and they cut pulpwood for Luke Mill," Diaz said.

They worked eight hours a day for pay. Prisoners received a portion of the pay in camp credit and the government got the rest to offset camp costs.

The prisoners ate the same food as the guards and sometimes worked as camp cooks. Their clothing was labeled with the letter P sewn on one pants leg and shirtsleeve and the letter W sewn on the other pants legs and shirtsleeve.

Bill Johnson, a forestry official during WWII, recalled in Land of the Living by John Mash, "We were never worried about the prisoners escaping. Guards were in the woods with them and the prisoners were afraid of getting lost, after all, they were in enemy territory."

Once, a guard fell asleep while watching POWs picking fruit in an orchard. One of the prisoners walked over to the snoozing guard.

"He got the guard's gun and did the German manual of arms and then gave it back to him," Diaz said.

And the guard never knew his rifle had been missing. The POWs considered it a great joke.

Such was life at Camp Flintstone. The guards were as hard on the prisoners as needed, but it wasn't often needed.

"The only problem I ever saw was a young punk," Diaz said. "He was hard and he wound up in solitary confinement for a week on bread and water. He wasn't performing. He wouldn't do anything."

One winter day while the POWs cut wood in the forest, a prisoner walked over to a guard and said something to him. The two walked away together over a hill.

"The next thing I know is I hear gunshots. BLAM! BLAM! BLAM! All work stopped and everybody came running to find blood on the snow. I didn't know what in the hell was happening," said Henry Smith, a Little Orleans work foreman, in Land of the Living.

Then they saw the guard in the trees. He and the prisoner were fine. The prisoner had seen a deer and asked the guard to shoot it. He did. The POWs butchered the deer and smuggled the venison into the camp in their lunch pails.

In their off time, prisoners wrote postcards home, attended church services, played soccer on the ball field next to the camp and even produced plays.

"I don't remember any incident of spying of sabotage at Camp

Flintstone," Boehm said in *Land of the Living*. "I don't know what good it would have done anyhow in such a small camp. Nothing would have changed the course of the war. Everyone was happy and content. We escaped the hell of the war. Each POW, even a fanatic at heart, was happy to be in a U.S. prison and not in Siberia."

When the war ended in 1945, the orders came to close the camp. Boehm recalled the prisoners reluctantly left. "Once more a truck came and chauffeured us around the orchard so we could say goodbye to the friends we left behind. We did not know what the future would bring when we left there. Still each one of us shook hands and were not ashamed of the tears we shed."

Once the prisoners collected their belongings, Diaz said, "We brought them in trucks to the train station, loaded them onto trains and off we went to Camp Shanks in New York."

Boehm and Diaz met again in 1988 as old friends rather than guard and prisoners.

Today, Camp Flintstone is the Green Ridge Youth Center for delinquent boys.

This article appeared in the August/September 2006 issue of Allegany Magazine.

Family desperately searches for woman's killer

When Odessa Meister said goodbye to her daughter Nancy as she left for work, neither knew that Odessa was truly saying goodbye because they would not see each other again.

On Dec. 20, 1952, Odessa left her home on Columbia Street around 1:50 p.m. and boarded the Cumberland Transit Lines bus to get to work. Odessa, 35, was an attractive woman. She had a slim build and dark complexion. People tended to notice her and at least two passengers and the bus driver remembered Odessa.

She got off the bus near the Celanese Plant on McMullen Highway. As she approached the gate, a car blew its horn at her. She stopped, approached the car and talked to the driver for a few moments. Then she climbed into the car and it drove away.

Odessa was never seen alive again and her final hours have never fully been accounted for.

"Two Flintstone brothers furnished authorities with a new lead. They told of collecting junk December 20 in the section where the body was found. As they passed an old model car bearing Maryland tags, the driver, a man, ducked down in the seat. A woman companion, they added, did likewise," reported the *Cumberland Evening Times*.

The brothers were Roy and Harry Dolly and the car they saw was a 1939 Buick painted a dark gray. They even made a point to remember the license number, but they forgot it by the time they realized they might have seen Odessa and her murderer.

Mrs. Glenn Ritchie reported seeing Odessa in the Lonaconing Republican Club the evening of the 20th. She said what struck her was that Odessa was wearing clothes that she usually wore to work and that she wore her hair down. Other people at the club weren't able to corroborate her story, though police considered it when trying to retrace Odessa's last hours.

How long after that she remained alive, no one knows.

After Odessa was missing for more than a week, a public cry for help was made by the family.

Annabelle Clem found Odessa's red purse in a wooded section of Park Avenue in Bowman's Addition about 1.5 miles from where her body would eventually be found. It was water-damaged so police suspected that it had been outside for awhile. It contained nothing but her Celanese Plant identification card.

Police Chief R. Emmett Flynn said, "It just doesn't look good for her. I don't like the pocketbook found in that lonely, desolate spot." He said that it looked especially bad because "a woman will hold onto her pocketbook to the last."

"With the spot of the pocketbook discovery serving as the focal point, the three score of searchers fanned out in all directions, the human tentacles reaching almost to the top of Wills Mountain," reported the *Cumberland Evening Times*. The search yielded a handkerchief and bobby pin, which were thought at the time to be clues.

As her days missing grew, rumors began to circulate that Odessa's body had been discovered. "The discovery was variously reported to have taken place at Lake Gordon, Lake Koon, on Wills, Haystack and Backbone mountains, on Braddock and Old Furnace roads and in Bowman's Addition," reported the newspaper.

As the new year came, the investigation stalemated. Without a body, there could be no crime.

Odessa's sister Virginia Farrin said, "The family all think she must have been killed. She never disappeared before and there is nothing in her life to explain it. She was devoted to her daughter and would hardly have left her at this season."

In desperation, Farrin even traveled to Richmond, Va., seeking the aid of Lady Wonder, a 27-year-old horse credited with telepathic powers that spells out her answers on a device resembling a modified typewriter. The first visit was unsuccessful but during a later visit the newspaper reported, "Mrs. Farrin said she asked whether Mrs. Meister were alive or dead and 'Lady Wonder,' spelled out D-E-A-D with a system of signs she manipulates. To a further question, 'Lady Wonder' said Mrs. Meister would be found in W-A-T-E-R and had been P-U-S-H-E-D."

The truth was even worse when Odessa's body was found the next day.

Odessa Meister

City woman's death remains a mystery

James Murphy and James Aiello, Fort Hill juniors, played hooky from school Jan. 16, 1953, to catch rabbits and check up on a dead dog buried on McNamee's Hill. They didn't find the dog, but they did make a discovery that people still remember.

As they passed by a pile of cardboard and old *Life* magazines, Murphy took a stray kick at the pile. The magazines shifted and a woman's feet wearing shoes appeared.

The boys ran to the home of Thomas Hammersmith on Forester Avenue and told Mrs. Hammersmith what they had seen. She phoned her brother Patrolman Gordon Hite and he called police headquarters.

The police uncovered the body and found Odessa Meister lying face down. She was clothed in her red and black plaid coat, a tan skirt and a scarf around her neck. It was the same clothes she had been wearing when she'd last been seen. Her coat was buttoned and her hands gloved. There were some snags in the front of her stockings that indicated to police that she may have been dragged a short distance after being beaten. Her right hand was above her head and her left was at her side.

The *Baltimore Sun* reported, "On the ground where the body was found there was a large amount of blood under the head, leading to the theory that Mrs. Meister was still alive or dead for only a short period when she was buried beneath the trash."

The *Cumberland Evening Times* reported that the boys' "discovery set off one of the most intensive murder investigations in recent memory, and the case immediately became one of the most widely discussed murders in Allegany County history."

Police believed that whoever took Odessa to the spot where her body was found was familiar with the area because the roadway led to a dead end and there was a path down the hillside between Leiper Street and Rosewood Avenue.

Allegany County Medical Examiner H.V. Deming estimated that Odessa had been dead 25 to 27 days when her body was found. That put her time of death between Dec. 21 and 23. She had been missing since Dec. 20. Dr. Benedict Skitarello conducted the autopsy at Memorial Hospital. He determined that Odessa had been struck eight times on the head with a blunt object. Most of the blows were on the left side and the back of the head.

"She died of a brain hemorrhage resulting from a skull fracture," the newspaper reported.

Odessa had not been raped. Her clothes had not been disturbed and there were no other marks on her. Her body was identified by her friend Carolyn Welsh and Patrolman Kenneth Morrissey, who knew Odessa.

The following day, the Rev. J. Lawrence Kilkenny at St. Patrick's Church conducted a Mass. Odessa was buried in the parish cemetery on a cold, bleak Saturday morning.

Three days after the body was found, the first suspect was taken into custody. He was questioned all day by investigators and then held for six days. Bayse Peddicord, 51, worked at the Celanese Plant, though he had been laid off in December. The newspaper reported that he was "romantically linked with Meister until it ended shortly before her death." He had tried to reconcile with her a number of times, which led to noisy arguments in the Celanese parking lot.

Because no charges were filed, Peddicord was freed Jan. 25. Upon his release, Peddicord borrowed a tie from a reporter and posed for pictures. Police sent out 182 letters to Celanese employees asking for information. Most of the responses amounted to nothing, but Cumberland Detective Lt. James Van received a threatening letter warning him to "lay off the Meister case or you're next."

Odessa's husband, Thomas, passed a lie detector test twice, which cleared him of having any knowledge of who had killed his wife. A pair of tortoise-shell bifocal glasses found near the body led to the police visiting optometrists to see if the prescription could be traced. Though Peddicord was known to have a pair of similar glasses, he didn't wear bifocals.

Police questioned area dry cleaners to see if someone had brought in clothes to have them cleaned of blood. Some clothing was found to be suspicious, but it was never discovered whether there was a connection between the clothing and any of the suspects. Police searched for a gold wrist watch Odessa had been wearing at the time but it was never found. Her wallet also was never found.

While Odessa's organs had been too decomposed for examination, her clothes were sent to the FBI.

On April 16, Charles Burkett, 41, was taken into custody. According to Allegany County State's Attorney Paul Fletcher, "Early in April,

Burkett told a service station attendant he knew where Mrs. Meister had been killed and that the spot was not where her body was found."

After two days of questioning, Burkett apparently confessed to the murder. His black Buick was impounded and the front seat removed to test some splotches on the material. Tests eventually showed the splotches were not human blood but red paint.

The state's attorney kept Burkett's whereabouts a tight secret. Family, his lawyer and the press all had trouble finding him. He was held at various times in the Washington County Jail, the Allegany County Jail and the Allegany County infirmary. Burkett's lawyer, Howard Naughton, said, "Mr. Fletcher showed me the entire file in the case and I am satisfied the state's attorney could have gotten a warrant for murder on the basis of Burkett's original statements."

Bill Baker was the county investigator at the time. He said that Burkett knew some things but other details were wrong. "He had made up the story because he was looking for publicity for himself."

Burkett was released after a week with no formal charges being filed against him. He sobbed upon his release. Baker still believes the murderer was Peddicord. "He and I went to the same church. Sometimes we would even sit in the same pew. I always hoped that someday, when he knew he was going to die, he would call me and give me a confession, but he never did," said Baker.

The murderer was never found nor was a murder weapon or motive ever discovered. The two boys who discovered Odessa's body were given a $100 reward by her father. They were also given 12 extra periods of detention for playing hooky.

These articles appeared in the Cumberland Times-News on September 12, 2004 and September 13, 2004.

Trumans draw a crowd in Frostburg during lunch stop

The elderly couple entered the Princess Restaurant in Frostburg on June 21, 1953, a pleasant summer day. They asked for a table where they could eat lunch. Grace Felker, one of the two waitresses at the restaurant, set the table, seated the couple and gave the couple their water.

She stared at them for a moment and then walked off as the couple considered their menus.

"Dorothy, who are those people over there? They look familiar,' Grace asked Dorothy Pappas, the restaurant owner's daughter-in-law.

Dorothy looked at the couple and her eyes widened. "That's the ex-president and his wife."

"Aw, you're kidding," Grace said.

At that moment, Harry Truman looked up and said, "No, she's not."

Harry and Bess Truman were on their way to Washington from their home in Missouri along U.S. Route 40. As lunch time approached, they found themselves in Frostburg and asked someone where to find a good place to eat. They were directed to the Princess Restaurant on Main Street owned by George Pappas.

"As the Trumans sat in a booth eating, word spread that the former president and first lady were in town. Townspeople started to drop in for a Coke, and one bystander estimated the restaurant did a bigger soft drink business in the time the Trumans were there than in any other similar period," reported the *Cumberland Evening Times*.

"In 20 minutes, the place filled up with all kinds of people," said George Pappas, grandson of the original owner.

Used to celebrity, the Trumans greeted everyone who approached them to shake their hands and welcome them to Frostburg. Youngsters asked for autographs and Harry graciously obliged.

Bill Byrnes, a state motor vehicles inspector and well-known Democrat, approached the former president and shook his hand. Then Bill told Harry that Elizabeth Byrnes, his mother, was a big fan of Harry's but she had been stuck in bed with a broken hip since April 1. He asked if they might stop and say hello to his mother since it was on their way to Washington.

After eating, the Trumans left the restaurant and climbed into their Chrysler. They drove down U.S. 40 to Eckhart and stopped in to see Elizabeth.

"Neighbors dropped in to be introduced to the Trumans and to sit on the Byrnes' front porch while Truman, at his folksy best, chatted and admired the mountain scenery," reported the *Cumberland Evening Times*.

"They were down there over an hour," George Pappas recalls.

Once the Trumans continued on their trip, they were also spotted in Cumberland at the intersection of Henderson Avenue and Valley Road.

When Elizabeth died a couple of months later, Harry sent Bill a short letter expressing the Trumans' sympathy.

"I am certainly sorry to hear it but I am more than happy that I had an opportunity to see her on my way to Washington," wrote Harry.

This article appeared in the Cumberland Times-News on June 21, 2004.

"It's a girl" three times

"It's a girl."

The doctor in the Memorial Hospital delivery room called out the words at 3:37 a.m. on May 4, 1955. They would soon have a familiar ring to them.

A pink, wiggling baby announced her birth to the world with a mewling cry. Her cry was matched by her 21-year-old mother, Ruth Irene Shroyer, as another labor pain hit.

The doctor cut the umbilical cord, tied it off and passed the baby to the nurse. He still had work to do.

Nine minutes later, the doctor again called out, 'It's a girl."

A second little girl joined her sister.

The second girl was not unexpected. When the obstetrician-gynecologist had been called in to cover for his Hyndman colleague who had provided Ruth with prenatal care, the nurse told him, "You can hear heartbeats everywhere."

Again, nine minutes later, the doctor announced, "It's a girl."

He passed the baby to the waiting nurse and marveled at what he had just seen. In his 14 years as a doctor, he had never delivered triplets or even seen a set born. They were so small!

Ruth sighed with relief. It had only been two hours since she had entered the hospital but she had been in labor far longer. Her husband, Roy, had driven her to Memorial as quickly as he could but it still took some time to get from Hyndman to Cumberland.

She was a mother!

Sally Ann, Sara Mae and Susan Arlene Shroyer were the first triplets born in Cumberland in 17 years.

Because they were so small, the triplets weren't weighed immediately but instead the nurse wrapped each of them in a pink blanket and placed them in a steel-and-glass incubator to keep them warm. At their first weighing, they tipped the scales at 2 pounds, 1 ounce.

Ruth Irene Shroyer holds one of her daughter Susan, the surviving Shroyer triplet, in 1955. Courtesy of Susan Ranker.

Though the *Cumberland Evening News* reported that the Shroyer girls weren't due until the first part of July, both the sisters and their mother were listed in good condition following the birth.

Roy realized he was 24 years old with a family of five to support on his pay as a laborer for Bethlehem Steel.

Three daughters!

It was almost unfathomable to him. He and Ruth told the newspaper they only had a "suspicion of twins."

But triplets!

The newspaper reported "joy and excitement predominated" as the Shroyers, their family and hospital staff celebrated the three new lives. That evening, one of the heartbeats you could hear everywhere stopped. Sara Mae died. She had been just too small to survive outside the safety of her mother's womb.

Even as Roy and Ruth mourned the loss of their daughter, Sally Ann died early the next morning.

Susan Arlene was left an only child without having known her sisters to an extent she would ever remember.

The graveside service for Sally and Sara was held at 10:30 a.m. the next day. The Rev. Charles Evans laid their tiny caskets in the ground of Comps Cemetery near Hyndman.

Susan remained in the hospital for 63 days as doctors worked to make sure she remained healthy. At one point, her weight dropped to 1 pound 14.5 ounces, but when she left the hospital, she weighed a solid 5 pounds.

Susan Shroyer is now Susan Ranker. She is married to Ray Ranker and still lives in Hyndman not far from where she grew up. They have three children and four grandchildren.

Susan said she thinks often about her sisters but she is still uncertain why she lived. "I figure God had a reason for wanting me to be here," Susan said.

While the Shroyers started off their family with a bang, Susan grew up an only child with no memory or picture of her sisters.

"Mom and Dad just were never able to have any more kids," said Susan.

Fortunately, the first triplets born at Memorial Hospital since it opened in August 1929 fared better. They were born in October 1938 to Harold L. Smith and his wife, who lived in Cumberland. Each of the girls weighed 5 pounds at the time.

By the time the Shroyer girls were born, the Smith girls were seniors at Allegany High and preparing to graduate as women.

This article appeared in the Cumberland Times-News on May 4, 2004.

Surprise guests

In 1962, the first year the National Transportation Safety Board began recording aircraft accidents, 331 people died in the United States in 64 incidents. In July, a flight to Honolulu crashed killing 127 passengers. In May, dynamite hidden in flight exploded a plane over Iowa killing 45 passengers.

Even if the flights weren't fatal, they could be scary. In August, a jet with 81 passengers landed in a field in Iowa instead of an airport "by mistake."

The Cumberland Municipal Airport escaped most of the accidents of this nature. Never a major passenger airport, the airport catered to smaller aircraft and lighter aircraft.

So it wasn't surprising that one clear Saturday night in 1962, Airport Manager John Nash called in 17-year-old James Abe of Wiley Ford to hold down the fort at airport. Nash had somewhere he needed to be so he had to leave early. Abe had been working at the airport part-time for about a year. All he was expected to do was be at the airport and turn on the runway lights if anybody came in.

And that's all he did, but in doing so, he helped keep that 331 fatalities in 1962 from climbing over 400.

Around 10:30 p.m., Abe took a call from Martinsburg Flight Service. He was told a TWA Martin 404 passenger flight on its way to Washington DC was going to make an emergency landing at the airport.

"Make sure the lights are on," the caller told Abe. "He's got an engine out and he's going to land."

Abe quickly turned on the runway lights. He also called the Cumberland police and fire departments. Then he went outside to sit on a bench and wait for the plane to land. Before long, he could see the plane coming in from the east.

The Martin 404 first came into service in 1950. The planes were about 75 feet long and 93 feet wide from wingtip to wingtip. They could also travel at 225 miles per hour, but this plane was only flying on one engine.

The plane intended on landing on runway 24, which was just over a mile long.

This Martin 404 is shown having an engine replaced at the Cumberland Municipal Airport after an emergency landing in 1962. Courtesy of Bill Armstrong and Bob Poling.

However, Abe quickly saw a problem as the plane drew closer. He remembers thinking, "Oh, my God, he's too high. He's never going to get it down and get it stopped."

Bob Poling and Bill Armstrong wrote in their book, *Wings Over Cumberland: An Aviation History*, "In any emergency of this kind, and especially at night on an unfamiliar airport with a twin engine airplane, pilots often add five or more knots airspeed to their approach air speed, as a safety factor against unexpected obstacles. However the Martin 404 was known as an aircraft that, with excessive airspeed, would float quite a bit upon round out for landing."

The plane had passed over more than half the runway before it finally touched down.

Abe was scared because if he knew if the plane couldn't stop in time, there was a 100-foot drop at the end of the runway and below that were houses. It looked like a disaster in the making.

"I thought, 'This is going to be awful. I don't want to see it,'" Abe said.

He started to go for help when he heard the reverse thrusters screeching. The plane quickly slowed down. When it finally stopped at the end of the runway, the nose gear sat in the grass.

As the plane taxied to the administration building, Abe felt a great weight lift off his shoulders.

"People started getting off the airplane," Abe said. "They did not know where the hell they were. The stewardesses tried to answer their questions and calm them down. Then they just started passing out the miniatures. That calmed them down a bit."

Poling and Armstrong write that the aircrew of the TWA flight got their first look at Wiley Ford and the mountain beyond the runway the plane had landed on the next morning.

"In the daylight hours the TWA pilots realized how lucky they were and had second thoughts about their high airspeed during their emergency approach into Cumberland," Poling and Armstrong wrote.

Runway 6/24 has since been replaced by runway 5/23. It has clearer approaches, though it is a shorter runway, according to Poling and Armstrong.

This article appeared in the Cumberland Times-News on February 27, 2007.

Crew jumps, B-52 crashes

"Mayday! Mayday! Mayday! Buzz one four is bailing out!"
Air Force Pilot Tom McCormick yelled into the radio trying to be heard above the gale-force winds. A clanging bell sounded throughout the B-52 Strato-Fortress that carried two thermonuclear warheads as it hurtled through the air upside down six miles above the earth in January 1964.

The bell and the blinking red light at each crew position told the five men that it was time to bail out. Just moments before, severe winds had ripped off the tail of the plane, taking the left horizontal stabilizer and tail gunners pod with it.

The B-52 slid sideways. Then its right wing slowly rose and turned the plane over with it, which began a lopsided spin. The g-forces of the spin alternately threw the crew back into their seats or straining against their harnesses.

Co-pilot Mack Peedin lost hold of the control wheel. A hatch blew as the crew prepared to eject. The warmth of the cockpit and oxygen vanished in an instant. Arctic air numbed any flesh it could find.

Then the airmen ejected. Peedin fell through the air for more than six minutes before finally landing on a farm two miles south of Grantsville. McCormick ejected and fell for more than 10 minutes before he landed on Meadow Mountain near the Maryland-Pennsylvania line. Mel Wooten, the tail gunner, was wounded when he ejected but he was alive when he landed on the Dye Factory Field in Salisbury, Pa. Navigator Robert Payne ejected and landed in a tree near New Germany State Park.

Bombardier Robert Townley stayed with the plane as it crashed into

Big Savage Mountain. It is believed that he was partially out of his harness when the plane's tail was lost. At that point, he was unable to refasten himself and eject.

Searchers for B-52 wreckage in the January 1964 in Garrett County would have been looking for a nuclear weapon similar to this one from a 1961 B-52 crash in North Carolina. Courtesy of Wikimedia Commons.

Jesse Green, who lived about a mile away, was the first person on the scene of the crash site. He couldn't get too close to the wreckage because it was burning and ammunition was firing off.

As news spread about the crash, people began to mobilize. Over the next five days, the county plowed the road up Big Savage Mountain. Phones were installed near the crash site and guards posted to keep the curious away. Salisbury (Pa.) Police Chief George Winters had a thousand volunteers combing the woods. Army and Civil Air Patrol aircraft circled the area searching for parachutes to identify where survivors had fallen.

A B-52 similar to this one was ripped apart in heavy winds over Garrett County in January 1964. Courtesy of Wikimedia Commons.

Quarry owner Ray Giconi got his men, a huge forklift and a couple of dump trucks to the crash site. They lifted the warheads into the truck beds lined with mattresses.

A newspaper reporter asked Giconi if he wasn't scared handling the bombs. Giconi said, "I do know that if they'd gone off, instead of being in the quarry business I'd have been in the gravel business."

McCormick made his way two miles to U.S. Route 40 and became the first survivor found when he knocked on Robert Warnick's door around 4 p.m. on Monday, Jan.13. Peedin used a signal mirror to flash a Civil Air Patrol plane Tuesday morning. The searchers brought help and found him in excellent condition.

On Tuesday evening, Townley's remains were located in the B-52. On Wednesday morning, Payne was located. He had tried to walk to safety unsuccessfully. Then he had tried to light a fire, but his fingers had been dead by then. Apparently, he was still alive when found but he died before he could receive help. Wooten's body was found Friday morning not far from his parachute.

The accident was the final straw for the Air Force. It changed the design of the B-52. By the end of the month, the Air Force ordered 8 feet shaved from the 156-foot length and strengthened the bulkhead that had allowed the tail to shear off. Besides interviews, a 1998 article by David Wood with Newhouse News Service also provided information for this story.

This article appeared in the Cumberland Times-News on January 14, 2004.

After nearly 40 years, Welch murder case still unsolved

Monday, May 17, 1965, was a sunny spring day - warm enough to dry clothes on the outside line. Wearing shorts and a short-sleeved blouse, 33-year-old Jean Welch, an attractive brunette, carried the wet clothes in a basket outside to hang them up on the clothesline around 1:30 p.m. Whether she caught the eye of her killer then or at some earlier time is unknown. What is known is that within half an hour she was dead.

Jean's apartment was at 1000 E. Oldtown Road. She lived there with her husband, Dale, and their three daughters.

On that Monday afternoon, neighbors sat across the street on the porch of their home, watching traffic zip by. While they saw plenty of cars pass the house, no one approached the front door on Oldtown Road.

Jean's 13-year-old daughter, Judy Woodson (her daughter from her first marriage) had gone off to school and Dale was playing golf at the Cumberland Country Club.

Jean wasn't alone in the apartment, though. Her other daughters, 2-year-old Loy Lee and 1-year-old Dee Dee, were home.

Two families also lived on the second floor of the apartment building. One family wasn't home, but someone was in the other apartment.

"One woman from the other second-floor apartment was at home and investigation revealed she had heard a knock on the Welch's side-door," reported the *Cumberland Evening Times*. The side door was located on New Hampshire Avenue and it was used more often by family and friends than the front door.

The drapes on the apartment's large picture window had been open when Jean was hanging clothes, but someone noticed that by 3 p.m. they had been pulled shut.

Judy returned home around 4 o'clock and found the apartment in a bit of a mess. She found Dee Dee strapped to her training potty in the back bedroom. Loy Lee was also in the apartment and upset.

"Mom!" Judy called.

No answer.

She looked in her mother's bedroom but it was empty. The door to the bathroom was closed. Was her mother in there? She knocked on the door.

"Mom?"

When there was still no answer, Judy opened the door. Her mother was inside. Jean was laying face down in a partially filled tub of water and not moving.

Judy screamed.

Dale Welch finished his round of golf around 4:15 p.m. and headed back to his office at Air-Flow Roofing and Siding Company where he was vice president.

"While en route from the golf course to the office, Mr. Welch was advised on his two-way car radio that there was 'an emergency' at his home," the *Cumberland Evening Times* reported.

Police were on the scene by the time he arrived. The deputy county medical examiner had examined the body and determined Jean had been killed by several blows to her head with a blunt instrument, but the murder weapon was nowhere to be found.

The killer also had gone to much trouble to make sure Jean was dead. Not only had he struck the killing blows, but also he had stran-gled her with the drapery cord and pushed her face down in the tub to drown her.

George Funeral Home conducted the funeral and Jean was buried in Sunset Memorial Park on Thursday.

Even before Jean was buried the rumors were flying fast and fu-rious about who the murderer was.

State's Attorney Donald Mason warned the public, "Persons who start or repeat these false rumors are subject to legal action for civil slander by persons whose names are mentioned. These false rumors also hinder the work of the investigating officers who are working tirelessly on this case."

In the last photo taken of Jean Welch, she holds her daughters, Loy Lee and Dee Dee, on her lap. Both girls were in the apartment with their mother when she was killed. The photo was taken just a few days before her death on May 17, 1965. Courtesy of Dee Bower.

The grapevine was more certain of the murderer than the police because they made no arrest, though they logged thousands of man-hours of leg work searching for the killer.

More than 300 people were questioned about what they had seen between noon and 5 p.m. on the day the crime occurred.

Cumberland Police Detective Capt. James Van and other officers stopped cars along Oldtown Road during the time period the murder might have occurred and questioned the drivers.

Police also searched diligently for the murder weapon. Garbage cans, backyards, sewers, vacant lots, fields, play and recreation areas were searched by police in the hopes of finding the weapon.

"The residents of Oldtown Road area have been cooperative and many have cut their lawns, trimmed their hedges seeking the murder weapon in an effort to assist police," reported the *Cumberland Evening Times.*

Also hindering the investigation was that the crime scene had been mishandled at the beginning, which resulted in the loss of valuable evidence such as blood samples and fingerprints.

"It wasn't that someone committed the perfect murder and got away with it. Things got messed up," said Loy (Welch) Capshaw.

Then Cumberland Police Chief B. Frank Gaffney told the newspaper, "As of now there has been no basic motive established and we are operating on all theories. The murderer could be a friend or stranger, local or transient."

Dale, who was a victim of some of the speculation, was among the dozen or so people who took a lie detector test administered by the Maryland State Police.

After the test, the newspaper reported, "The investigating officials have issued a report on the findings of the polygraph testing which states he (Dale) had no knowledge of any facts relating to the death of his wife." Later tests yielded the same results.

At the investigation's peak, 10 officers were assigned full-time to the case with many other people from different agencies looking at it on a part-time basis.

Sylvester J. Smith, president of the Air-Flow Roofing and Siding Company, offered a $1,000 reward for information leading to the capture of Jean's killer.

No arrests were made, though, and the case turned cold. According to Bill Baker, the county investigator at the time, police had a good idea of who the killer was but they just never had enough evidence to take the case to trial.

When the trail began to turn cold, Dale himself offered a $5,000 reward for information leading to the capture of the murderer. No one came forward with the needed information.

Three young girls had to grow up without their mother and Dale spent most of the rest of his life trying to keep the case active.

"As I got older and my sisters got older, it was almost as if my mother had never lived," said Capshaw.

For Dale, it was the opposite. Years after the murder, he would still say "it seemed like it happened yesterday."

In the 39 years since the murder, the murderer has not been found and the case remains unsolved today.

This article appeared in the Cumberland Times-News on August 8, 2004.

Washington a favorite uncle

If Cumberland has a favorite uncle, it would have to be George Washington. Though Washington did not build Fort Cumberland or name it, he was serving with Gen. Edward Braddock when he entered the newly constructed fort in 1755.

That surely earns him "uncle" status. And just like a favorite uncle, he visited his niece at different times, including ending his military career here. Because Washington is so closely tied to Cumberland's history, it was no surprise that when the city wanted to present its first Heritage Days in 1969, the residents chose Washington's birthday, Feb. 22.

"Washington's birthday is a unique opportunity for Cumberland to celebrate this date in our nation's history," Operation Gateway President Juanita Isiminger told the *Cumberland Evening Times* on the eve of the first Heritage Days.

The idea for Heritage Days began with Operation Gateway, a volunteer organization that was created to promote civic and historic pride. It was formed in 1968, when Isiminger of the Women's Civic Club requested that the organization add a committee that would promote civic pride, the area's rich history and the scenic beauty of the region.

Isiminger served as president of Operation Gateway and would continue to do so until her death in 1978.

The events on Saturday, Feb. 22, began with a pancake breakfast at the Elks Club #63 on South Centre Street. Throughout the day groups were taken on tours by guides wearing black-and-orange armbands. The guides showed some of the historic buildings in the city, including City Hall, the Fort Cumberland tunnels, George Washington's Headquarters, History House and the Masonic Temple. The Women's Civic Club hosted a luncheon at its club house on Washington Street.

In the afternoon, there were drills and a relic display by the 2nd Maryland Regiment of the Maryland Line at Washington's headquarters. An early forge supplied by the Baltimore and Ohio Railroad was also in operation in the park. Then at 1:30 p.m. and 3:30 p.m. there was an original historical pageant at Prospect Square. "Washington at the Western Frontier" was written by Joy Douglas and staged by the Algonquin Players under the direction of Jane Schwab.

Dinner was at the Shrine Club followed by a dance at the Elks Club. The toastmaster for the dinner was Winfield H. Adams, and Maj. Christopher Willoughby of the British Embassy gave the address. The Chip N Dippity Singers provided the music for the event. Other guests included Lt. Col. E.H. McDonald, military representative of the governor of Virginia; Col. Randolph Millholland, military representative of the governor of Maryland; and Cumberland Mayor Thomas Conlon.

According to the Cumberland Evening Times, "The day's schedule attracted thousands to various events and the downtown 'Birthday Sales' added to the total. Lines formed outside the headquarters building and waited to tour the tunnels under Emmanuel Episcopal Church."

Operation Gateway even received a telegram from President Richard Nixon and Secretary of the Interior Walter Hickle that said in part, "You have chosen an interesting and constructive way to observe this historic occasion."

The current Heritage Days bears little resemblance to that first one 35 years ago but it still continues to arouse citizens and remind them of the beauty and history of the area.

This article appeared in the Cumberland Times-News on June 11, 2004.

About the Author

James is the author of seven novels. These include the historical novels *Canawlers, October Mourning, Between Rail and River* and *The Rain Man*. His other novels are *Logan's Fire, Beast* and *My Little Angel*.

He works as a freelance writer who lives in Gettysburg, PA. Jim has received numerous awards from the Maryland-Delaware-DC Press Association, Associated Press, Maryland State Teachers Association and Community Newspapers Holdings, Inc. for his newspaper writing.

If you would like to be kept up to date on new books being published by James or ask him questions, he can be reached by e-mail at *jimrada@yahoo.com*.

To see James' other books or to order copies on-line, go to *www.aimpublishinggroup.com*.